Beyond th

Beyond the plc

Greg Fisher
and
Paul Ormerod

Civitas: Institute for the Study of Civil Society
London

First Published May 2013

© Civitas 2013
55 Tufton Street
London SW1P 3QL

email: books@civitas.org.uk

ISBN 978-1-906837-53-2

Independence: Civitas: Institute for the Study of Civil
Society is a registered educational charity (No. 1085494)
and a company limited by guarantee (No. 04023541).
Civitas is financed from a variety of private sources
to avoid over-reliance on any single or small group
of donors.

All publications are independently refereed. All the
Institute's publications seek to further its objective of
promoting the advancement of learning. The views
expressed are those of the authors, not of
the Institute.

Typeset by Kevin Dodd
Printed in Great Britain by
Berforts Group Ltd
Stevenage SG1 2BH

Contents

Authors

Greg Fisher is the Managing Director of Synthesis. After growing up in the West Midlands, he studied Economics & Politics at St John's College, University of Cambridge. Greg joined the Bank of England as a graduate entrant in 1995 and subsequently worked in a spectrum of roles that mixed economics and finance. Between 2004 and 2008, Greg worked for a hedge fund as a global macroeconomic strategist. Before joining the think-tank, ResPublica, in August 2010, he spent two years researching the new science of complex systems, and how it relates to economics and finance. Greg is a Senior Research Associate of the London School of Economics' Complexity Group. His interests extend beyond pure economics, and include human psychology, neuroscience and cognitive science, and how these relate to our understanding of society.

Paul Ormerod is a Director at Synthesis. He is the author of three best-selling books on economics, *Death of Economics* (1994), *Butterfly Economics* (1998), *Why Most Things Fail* (2005), a *Business Week* US Business Book of the Year. He read economics at Cambridge and took the MPhil in economics at Oxford. He worked initially as a macro-economic forecaster and modeller at the National Institute of Economic and Social Research in London. In the early 1980s he moved to the private sector as Director of Economics at the Henley Centre for Forecasting. The management team bought this from the Henley Management College and subsequently sold it to Martin Sorrel's WPP Group. He founded Volterra Consulting in 1998 in order to carry out innovative work on practical policy questions in both the public and private sectors. In 2009 he was awarded an honorary DSc by Durham for the 'distinction of his contributions to economics'.

He publishes on complexity-related areas in a wide range of academic journals such *as Proceedings of the Royal Society B(iology), Journal of Cultural Economics* and the *Journal of Economic Interaction and Co-ordination.*

Acknowledgments

We would like to thank a number of people who took part in meetings and a Round Table discussion during the life of the project. This included:

Arthur Batram (Plexity)
Jo Casebourne (NESTA)
Orit Gal (Regent's College)
Rhett Gayle (Synthesis)
David Green (Civitas)
Stephen Lloyd (Bates Wells & Braithwaite)
Mark McKergow (The Centre for Solutions Focus at Work)
Eve Mitleton-Kelly (London School of Economics)
Yasmin Merali (Warwick University)
Peter Morris
Jesse Norman MP
Sue Richards
Hank Sohota

In addition, we would like to thank Mark McKergow and Bridget Rosewell for commenting on earlier versions of the paper, in addition to two anonymous referees, and we would like to thank Kritvi Kedia who undertook the research that formed Appendix 1.

Most of all we would like to thank David Green, Director of Civitas, for supporting "next generation" economic thinking.

Executive Summary

The economy should be thought of as an evolutionary process rather than a static machine. Unfortunately, most of the economics taught in schools and universities frames the economy more like the latter than the former. This broad approach is also frequently used to formulate government policy, creating tension because economic institutions and policies ultimately become obsolete. *Organisational forms*, which are the legal entities that organisations may take, like joint stock companies and charities, are examples of institutions that can become obsolete if the legislative process concerned with such forms does not account for the evolution of the economy.

This book is written from a different and new approach to understanding the economy, orientated around the new study of dynamic networks (or complex systems). The book uses non-technical language, but we draw on what is now a deep literature in this field. This approach helps us to look at the economy as an evolving process rather than a machine full of automaton parts. Organisational forms include joint stock companies, companies limited by guarantee, charities, and community interest companies, among others. The main protagonist in our story is the joint stock company i.e. a limited liability company with shares publicly listed on a public stock exchange. This is by far the most dominant form of organisational form in the West today.

Organisations and Organisational Forms

In discussing organisational forms, we start by asking *why do organisations exist at all?* We address this issue in the second chapter, drawing on psychology studies, *Organisation Theory* and Sociology to get to the bottom of this. We conclude that organisations exist, first, to *integrate the work of specialists*, which is the basis of an *efficient*

1

organisation (this is a well-known conclusion in Organisation Theory); and, second, to *enable creativity*, which is the basis of a *resilient* organisation. This discussion fits neatly into our overarching framework of dynamic networks: successful organisations need to be efficient to survive in the moment but also resilient to survive over time, by adapting appropriately in the face of uncertainty and change.

The next question we concern ourselves with is *why do different forms of organisation exist?*

The third chapter of the book is spent describing some important history of various organisational forms. We focus on partnerships, joint stock companies, industrial and provident societies, co-operatives, charities, and community interest companies. In the new field of dynamic networks, it is important to look at such history to recognise patterns and, where possible, to draw useful conclusions. Chapter 4 draws out some key patterns from the empirical discussions of Chapter 3. An important conclusion we reach is that different organisational forms *establish the rights & responsibilities of all of the stakeholders concerning an organisation, in order to mitigate uncertainty for those stakeholders.*

Moreover, the suitable form of an organisation will vary depending on the part of the economy it operates in and the values it holds. For example, the joint stock company is broadly suited to industrial activity, partnerships are suited to some service-based organisations like accounting firms, and a community interest company is suited to firms seeking to add value to a community.

The Evolution of Forms

If we think about the economy as an evolutionary process, it is useful to compare organisational forms with species in an ecosystem. In evolution, species emerge and flourish if they are suitable to their environmental context. But over a long enough period of time, their contexts will change and species will either survive by adapting or they will become extinct.

One of the key policy recommendations in this book is that an important role for the government is to ensure that the set of organisational forms – or species – in the economy is relevant to the current and expected future economic environment (to the extent the latter is possible). It can do this by ensuring the statutory process concerned with organisational forms is, like the economy as a whole, evolutionary in nature, thereby maintaining a portfolio of forms which are relevant and useful to people in the economy today. The community interest company is an excellent case study of the creation of a new form that was appropriate to the economy ten years ago and remains so today. But this was, in effect, the only new form of organisation to have emerged over the past 150 years.

The Joint Stock Company

Given the importance of maintaining a set of relevant and useful forms, in Chapter 5 we take a closer look at the joint stock company. We do this for two reasons. First, the joint stock company is clearly the dominant species in the economic ecosphere today, so it is important in its own right; and, second, we use this as an example of the type of analysis required by government to ensure that the forms available to people are relevant. We ask a number of questions: Is the joint stock company still relevant today? How do we resolve some of the problems attributable to it? By re-designing it? By allowing it to become extinct? Or by allowing new forms to emerge that might, in effect, compete against it.

In discussing the problems of the joint stock company, we look at various issues of governance, notably the dilution of control over the executive by the Board of Directors and the company's shareholders. This topic is a well-trodden path but, nonetheless, we add to this debate by recommending that:

- Executives are rewarded not on the basis of the absolute share price performance of a company's stock (as with stock options) but on some measure of its relative share price performance e.g. relative to some appropriate index.

- The Financial Policy Committee requires all asset managers either to actively engage in shareholder affairs directly (i.e. voting) or to lodge their shares with shareholder proxy firms (who vote on their behalf). Furthermore, we would actively encourage collusion among shareholders and their proxy firms. These recommendations are essential to help overcome a free-rider problem inherent in investment management, which leads to (understandably) apathetic shareholders.

- Investment managers are barred from holding non-executive positions in any company, with the exception of private equity managers holding such positions in the companies in which they are invested. If they hold non-executive positions, investment managers have an incentive – albeit indirect – to maintain high rates of pay for such roles.

- The part of the Companies Act 2006 dealing with social and environmental impact (Part 10, Section 172) is properly enforced. In Chapter 5 we recommend a slight rewording of this section of the Act but the main thrust of our recommendation is for existing law to be better enforced. Moreover, we would recommend that if directors fail to carry out their duties, it is the companies in which they work that are prosecuted, not the directors personally.

In addition to looking at the joint stock company, in Chapter 5 we discuss the principle of limited liability, which is a key feature of joint stock companies (and other forms). We make a specific recommendation that:

- Companies with limited liability are required to take out insurance to protect their business counterparts against default, equivalent to third-party car insurance. The rationale for this is due to limited liability creating a moral hazard for companies whereby they will take risks greater than if their liabilities were not limited. They are already insured by limited liability so we argue that they be required to pay a counterpart insurance premium.

Moreover, in line with the overall thrust of the book, we recommend that an important response to the problems which have emerged with the joint stock company is to allow for the creation of new forms, examples of which include:

- A triple bottom line company, which fits with a wider set of values i.e. beyond profit maximisation, to include social and environmental impact;

- A new form with a German-style governance structure; and

- A new banking form to capture the fact that banks play a unique role in the economy. We also recommend that banks pay a much greater banking levy to the government. This would be an insurance premium counterpart to the insurance they clearly receive from the government when they become insolvent or illiquid.

The New Economy

In Chapter 6, we move from looking at 'the old' to looking at 'the new' by conducting a pattern recognition process of some of the emerging themes in the digital economy. This type of analysis also needs to happen on a perpetual basis, to ascertain whether new organisational forms would be useful. We argue that networked computers are leading to both a newly emerging digital economy and also to an evolution in older parts of the economy. This is significant and we argue that certain fundamental principles of traditional economics, such as scarcity and the division between production and consumption, are being challenged as a result. There has also been an apparent intensification of mass collaboration in recent years e.g. Wikipedia. In looking at the new economy, we draw from the P2P Foundation, which provides a useful analysis of the new economy and also proposes a brand new organisational form, the *for-benefit organisation*.

One of the many parts of the new economy is the co-construction of commonly used software. 'Distributed enterprises' can help with the *creation and evolution* of commonly developed software (like Linux) but they also *use* this software at the same time. The P2P Foundation has argued that a new organisational form is needed to protect co-constructed assets like software architecture, and thereby support its development. Examples like Linux, which are in essence digital institutions, have emerged in spite of the lack of such a new form.

We recommend that:

- The government (specifically, the Department for Business, Innovation and Skills (BIS)) considers a new organisational form specifically for the purpose of developing and protecting such co-created assets.

Conclusion

In the concluding chapter we re-iterate policy recommendations noted above. In addition, we recommend:

- Simplifying and tidying up the complicated legislation concerned with organisation forms by drafting a single

Incorporation Act, by which all incorporated organisations must abide. Each incorporated form can also be bound by a second piece of legislation, which is specific to its type e.g. a new Charities Act stripped of its incorporation details. This approach would help the government to ensure that legislation concerned with all incorporated organisations evolves, helping to retire and adapt older forms, and create new forms.

- BIS is tasked with leading a perpetual 'conversation' with the evolving economy in order to ascertain the current nature of the economy and how it was expected to evolve. This is in order to question whether existing organisational forms were relevant and whether new forms (like the for-benefit organisation) were warranted. It is important that BIS does not fully own this process – it must be done in open conversation with participants in the economy.

In the final section of Chapter 7 we ask the essential question of whether the advantages of the approach we have proposed in this book outweigh the costs. We believe they do. We are not recommending a new set of unnecessary, bureaucratic statutes; rather we advise the operation of a statutory process that is evolutionary in the same way that the underlying economy is. We do not think the direct financial costs will be significantly different to the costs incurred in the current approach, in a steady state. In fact, we think that the simplification of legislation, with a single Incorporation Act, in addition to a detailed statute for each organisational form, will ultimately reduce costs.

The greatest benefit, however, will be to those involved with organisations. We argue in chapters 3 & 4 that the role of statutes concerned with organisational forms is to mitigate (not eliminate) the uncertainty faced by stakeholders. In the face of an increasingly complex global economy undergoing rapid . technological change, maintaining a portfolio of statutes to mitigate business uncertainty would be beneficial to the UK economy.

1

The Thesis

The corporate world exhibits a wide variety of structures. Co-operatives and partnerships have been around for a long time and some of them are well-known. *The Co-op*, for example, was founded in Rochdale as long ago as 1844 and is now represented worldwide. Goldman Sachs was a partnership for most of its existence. There are more exotic forms of the corporate beast, such as companies limited by guarantee, industrial and provident societies, friendly societies and, recently made possible by legislation in the UK, community interest companies.

But by far the dominant form of corporate organisation is that of the joint stock company. In other words, companies ultimately controlled by shareholders with publicly listed shares. These can range from one-person bands to the world's largest firms such as Google. This book is an investigation of the different forms of organisation that make up our economic system. At the heart of our thesis is that it is important for us to move from a broadly *static* view of the economy and its constituent organisations to a *dynamic* view of these things. At first blush, this might seem like a trivial distinction but when we delve deeper into the analysis, we find that a dynamic – or evolutionary – view of organisational forms has important implications for public policy.

On the whole, a static view of the economy leads policy to focus on the private and publicly listed companies and to frequently tinker with the Companies Act as the economy evolves. The metaphors of evolution and natural selection are useful here because in effect what we argue in this book is that different organisational forms are equivalent to species within an ecosphere. The role of public policy in this is to ensure that new, relevant species of organisation are allowed to emerge as the economy evolves and that older, more obsolete organisational forms are allowed to die.

The current, broadly static, view of the economy means that many of the organisational forms existing today are obsolete or outdated; and it means that we are missing a number of essential species, some of which are proposed or supported in this book. For example, we support the creation of a new organisational form that would aid the co-construction and protection of common resources like open source software (Linux being the quintessential example) and physical assets such as forests. We believe that if the approach to policy we propose here is put in to effect, it will lead to the UK having an ecosphere of relevant organisational species which compete against each other: a sort of meta-competition existing above competition among specific organisations. The result would be a healthy range of organisations which remain relevant to an evolving economic system.

A Brief History of Organisational Forms

In medieval Europe corporate law already recognised some institutions (cities, merchant and craft guilds, charitable entities) as legal corporations (distinct entities with legal personality). The practice of dividing ownership over tangible sources of wealth such as mines and ships was also widespread from the 14th and 15th centuries onwards.

However, the earliest recognisably modern companies with multiple shareholders were established in the 17th century, and were particularly concerned with trade in new colonial territories (for example, the British East India Company). In 1602, the Dutch East India Company first issued shares which owners could trade on the Amsterdam

Stock Exchange. This enhanced the ability of joint-stock companies to attract capital from investors as they were now easily able to dispose of their shares. This structure came to be seen as more financially viable than old guild systems and state-regulated companies. The number of companies like this was limited for some time, however, as incorporation was only permitted by Royal Charter or by an act of parliament.

The number of companies was also limited due to early lessons of the danger of stock over-inflation. While the British East India Company was financially successful, a similar company chartered to trade in South America, the South Sea Company, was the cause of the first 'speculative bubble' Britain had experienced. Company promoters were so successful in marketing shares that the price inflated far beyond the amount of trading and business being done, leading, when the bubble burst, to bankruptcy. Public sentiment moved strongly against corporations and the *Bubble Act 1720* prohibited the establishment of new corporations until 1825. Adam Smith wrote in *The Wealth of Nations* in 1776 that large-scale corporate activity could not match private entrepreneurship for generating lasting wealth, as people in charge of others' money (i.e. executive directors) would not exercise as much care with it as with their own. Today this is more commonly referred to in economics as the 'Principal-Agent problem'.

During the industrial revolution capital-intensive enterprises expanded rapidly and were generally operated as unincorporated associations or large extended partnerships. In effect, and speaking in broad terms, what happened during the industrial revolution was that the scale of economic production increased and moved well beyond the local level. When an economy is highly localised, traditional reputational effects and tacit information exchange can help to mitigate fraudulent behaviour. However, as economic networks broaden, the problem of 'information asymmetry' becomes more prevalent, which means potential investors cannot use traditional information channels to ascertain the investment worthiness of individuals or companies.

Legal change was required to facilitate business activity and regulation to prevent scams and protect investors in larger scale businesses. In the UK, the need for clarification of the legal standing and responsibilities of companies led to the following important legislation being introduced:

- *The Joint Stock Companies Act 1844*: allowed ordinary groups of people to register and incorporate capital enterprises. This meant incorporation no longer required an act of parliament or a Royal Charter.

- *The Limited Liability Act of 1855*: granted limited liability to companies of more than 25 shareholders.

- *The Joint Stock Companies Act 1856*: established limited liability for all joint-stock companies provided they include the word 'limited' in their name, allowing investors to limit their liability upon a company's default to the amount which they invested.

After the *Joint Stock Companies Act 1856*, a series of companies acts up to the current *Companies Act 2006* have refined the legal processes involved but these two fundamental features have been retained: recognition of the company as an individual under the eyes of the law and limited liability. The limited liability company has been by far the most dominant form of corporate structure for over a hundred years. The Appendix to this book sets out in detail the wide variety of forms which such structures can take in the UK today. But, according to the Office for National Statistics, there are just over 2 million trading enterprises in the UK[1], and of these some 60 per cent are companies. Sole proprietors, enterprises involving just a single person, make up almost 25 per cent of the total. The third largest group is partnerships, accounting for just over 10 per cent of enterprises. Together, these three forms constitute some 95 per cent of the total number of enterprises in the UK.

But the dominance of this particular 'species', the limited liability company, is dramatically more marked in terms of its economic importance. Precise figures are not readily available, as the Appendix points out. However, it is safe to say that companies with over 250 employees, which are almost exclusively limited liability companies, account for well over half of total private sector activity in the UK.

Static and Dynamic Views of the World

The above description is largely a static snapshot of the world of economic enterprises today within their historical context. But the real success of the limited liability company is that it has been the main structural vehicle for the tremendous success of capitalism in the 20th century. During the course of the century, for example, real income per head rose by some 350 per cent in the UK, 540 per cent in the US and 570 per cent in Germany. Over the same period, leisure time expanded dramatically. So, for example, average annual hours worked are estimated to have fallen by 44, 41 and 46 per cent in the UK, US and Germany respectively.[2] Annual holiday entitlement has also expanded. As late as the 1950s it was not uncommon for workers to have just a single week of holiday (in addition to public holidays), whereas at least four weeks is now the norm, certainly in the UK and on the Continent.

A critical period was the decades immediately around 1900. The combination of limited liability and the technological innovations of the telephone and the telegraph enabled the creation of enterprises operating on a hitherto unimagined scale. As the Harvard economic historian Alfred Chandler points out in his magnum opus, *Scale and Scope: the Dynamics of Industrial Capitalism*, the late 19th and early 20th century saw the creation of multi-national companies, as we recognise them today, for the first time. This was when the world economy first became truly globalised. A large number of the companies which were to become household names in the United States in the twentieth century grew rapidly around this time and established their market positions: Quaker Oats, Campbell's Soup, Heinz, Procter & Gamble, Schlitz and Anheuser Brewing, Eastman Kodak, American Telephone and Telegraph, Singer, Westinghouse, and Union Carbide. In addition to the new technologies enabling the creation of massive firms – US Steel, for example, employed over 200,000 workers – there was a huge wave of mergers and acquisitions in the decade 1895-1905. Just over 3,000 firms, many of substantial size, disappeared because of mergers. And the value of the consolidated firms which emerged as a result totalled almost $7 billion, or well over $1,000 billion in today's prices.

It is useful in the context of the themes of this book to consider the role of legislation in this merger and acquisition phenomenon and the evolution of corporate structure. The closing decades of the 19th century saw rapid technological change in many industries. Firms at the cutting edge reduced prices dramatically. Synthetic dye may sound dull and boring, but it was one of the late 19th century's equivalents to the information and communications technology (ICT) of our own times. The German dye manufacturers, Bayer, Hoechst and BASF were able to reduce the price of a new synthetic dye from 270 marks a kilo in 1869 to just 9 marks by 1886. Less efficient producers were simply swept aside.

A widespread response, in both Europe and America, to this unprecedented intensification of competition was to make formal agreements between companies, enforced by trade associations. Chandler noted that in the American hardware industry alone, which had many highly specialised product lines, no fewer than fifty trade associations managed the market for firms. These associations set quotas for output, fixed prices, and allocated different regions to different companies. The level of competition and innovation threatened the very existence of many firms, and the initial response was to band together to manage and control this frightening new beast. Competition gave way to collaboration.

But the policy of attempting to manage competition through cartels organised by trade associations failed pretty quickly. Essentially, there was no effective mechanism of policing the agreements on prices and output. Each individual member of an industry cartel faced a strong incentive to secretly cut prices to gain business. And once one firm had broken ranks, the others were compelled to follow suit, if they could. The less efficient were forced out of business because they were unable to make profits at the new, lower levels of price, and profits were lower than they were for those who survived.

It was always tempting for an individual firm to break the cartel, with the eventual result that all participants in the agreement ended up worse off. This revealed an age-old conflict between what we can think of as individual and collective rationality. It was in the collective interests of firms to maintain the cartel, but individual firms often came to believe that they themselves would be better off by breaking it. This failure of the structure within individual industries was soon reinforced in the United States by powerful statutory pressure. The Sherman Antitrust Act of 1890 not only made such combinations illegal, but provided the federal government with the authority to enforce this through the courts. The next response from industry was a massive wave of mergers and acquisitions, in which many companies simply disappeared into huge new conglomerates. The attempt to deal with the intensity of competition by forming trade associations to police behaviour had failed. Instead, competition was simply reduced by firms eliminating rivals by merging them into a single organisation.

In part, this dramatic reduction in the number of major players in each market was triggered by another piece of legislation, the general incorporation laws passed by the state of New Jersey in 1889. Astute business people realised that they provided a way round the fundamental problem facing trade associations; namely, the incentive for any individual member to renege in secret on the deal, and to cut its prices. Essentially, the New Jersey laws permitted the formation of holding companies, which gave firms the means with which to enforce legally the intra-firm agreements on prices and output. Legislation here played a decisive influence in the evolution of companies. However, it is important to recognise that the incentives created by legislation – to reduce competition by merger and acquisition – were completely compatible with fundamental aspects of business development at the time.

In much of economic theory, size is not just irrelevant but a definite handicap. A concept known as 'diminishing returns' prevails as an assumption in a lot of theory, so that as more labour and more capital are used in the production of a particular good or service, the extra output obtained from each additional unit input eventually falls. This assumption is not made on the basis of empirical evidence. It is made because it makes the maths, hard enough as they are, much more tractable and easier to handle analytically. But, historically, increasing returns have been widespread.[3]

Companies often gain distinct advantages through utilising economies of scope and scale in their operations, especially those with large capital outlays like industrial plants. As they get bigger, unit costs often fall, not rise.

Ironically, at the very same time that the concept of diminishing marginal returns was capturing the academic discipline of economics, the United States was moving towards world economic dominance by exploiting the unprecedented and massive increasing returns to scale of production, distribution and sourcing which its rapidly expanding economy permitted. In other words, US companies grew to dominance by taking advantage of the benefits of being big. In short, the technologies of the time enabled the creation of giant firms. The overall economic environment encouraged such creation. And legislation played an important role in motivating them to move in this direction.

An Evolutionary Perspective on Firms and Corporate Structure

Looking back at this period and the subsequent experience of the giant firms which were created, we can see clearly that for individual companies, the environment in which they operate is evolutionary, or highly dynamic. Firms, even giant ones, die, and new firms are born all the time. The economic historian Leslie Hannah charted what happened to the world's largest industrial companies in 1912.[4] The companies in the world's top 100 in 1912 represented the cream of capitalism. These were the survivors of a brutal era of competition, and had successfully survived the massive wave of mergers around the turn of the century. As Hannah pointed out: 'They were, on the whole, firms that contemporary stock market analysts considered attractive and safe because of their consistently reliable record of generous but sustainable dividends. A population of the largest firms of ten years earlier would almost certainly show earlier exits and faster rates of decline than this population.'

In short, these were the blue chip companies of their time. The value of the smallest, in stock exchange prices of 2004, was $5 billion, and of the largest $160 billion. Yet within 10 years, 10 of them had disappeared as independent concerns. By 1995, 29 of the 100 had experienced bankruptcy, another 48 had disappeared in other ways, and only 19 survived in the top 100. More generally, the evolution of individual companies has close empirical parallels with the evolution of individual biological species.

With the latter, palaeontologists have carried out painstaking analysis of the fossil record over the past 500 million years or so. They divide this enormous time span into some 80 different epochs, and estimate the percentage of all existing species that became extinct in each one of them. There are a small number of periods in which the extinction rate was very high. Around 65 million years ago, for example, with the disappearance of the dinosaurs. The most dramatic was the Permian extinction of some 250 million years ago, when over 90 per cent of the species existing at that time became extinct. But in most periods, the extinction rate is small. If we plot the size of an extinction event – the percentage of species becoming extinct – against the frequency of events of this size, we observe a well-defined mathematical relationship. If we take Les Hannah's data for the 100 largest non-financial companies in the world in 1912 and plot the size and frequency of extinctions (see Figure 1), this tells us that over the period 1912-1995, in most years – just over 50 in fact – none of these companies disappeared. The next most frequent 'size' was for one of them to become extinct in a particular year. Reading onto the left-hand axis of the bar above the number '1' on the bottom axis, we see that this

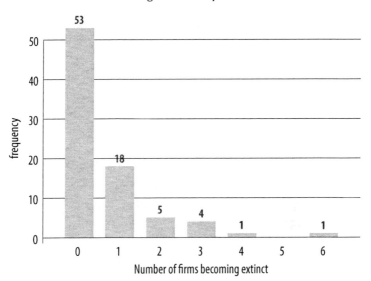

*Figure 1. Frequency of annual extinction rates 1912-1995
World's largest 100 companies in 1912*

was observed nearly 20 times. On the far right of the chart, we see an 'extreme event'; a year when no fewer than six of these firms vanished.

Of course, there are relatively few firms in this database, and we have to be careful in making too many claims for the particular structure of the relations between the size of an extinction event and its frequency. Remarkably, however, when we examine large modern databases of firms, segmenting by year, location and industry type, we see a very similar mathematical pattern. Occasionally, we see very high death rates of firms – the percentage becoming extinct – in a segment. For the most part, however, in any given segment, extinction rates are low.[5] And with large databases, we can be more confident about the nature of the relationship we observe empirically. As already mentioned, it is remarkably similar to that seen in the fossil record on the extinction patterns of biological species.

This prompts the question as to whether we might observe a similar phenomenon in the *types* of corporate structure which we observe. The great English economist Alfred Marshall, who established the Cambridge economics faculty in the late 19th century, was of the opinion that biology and not physics would ultimately prove to be by far the best inspiration for economics. His *Principles of Economics*, first published in 1890, was the dominant textbook in the early decades of the 20th century, and Marshall repeated his phrase that biology is the 'Mecca of the economist' in the Preface of every edition from the fifth onwards. In terms of the evolution of individual firms, we have seen there are close, and surprising, similarities between the extinction patterns of firms and of biological species. Might this exist for corporate structures? Whilst in theory it might, in practice the data do not allow us to test the hypothesis. The limited liability firm has been the dominant form of corporate structure, as we have seen, for at least a century. However, there is a further close potential parallel between the corporate world and that of biology. And this time it relates directly to corporate structure.

If we examine the relative frequencies with which the different types of structure are observed – even on a simple head count – we observe a highly skewed outcome. Huge numbers of shareholder-based companies, a lot of partnerships – but far fewer than the number of the 'market leader', some co-ops, then fewer and fewer until we get down to recent innovations such as the community interest company, with very few examples. The relationship is in fact similar, though not identical, to the one we observe in the extinction patterns of individual firms. Classic Darwinism would lead us to believe that the shareholder company is dominant because it is better suited to the environment, to the ecology of corporate structure. It is somehow fitter than its rivals. Importantly, however, we now know that selection by fitness does not by itself account for the relative frequencies with which we observe the different corporate forms.

A quite different theory also comes from biology, to account for the frequencies with which different species are observed in any given ecology. Stephen Hubbell, based at the University of California at Los Angeles, came up with the so-called 'neutral' theory, which generates results which conform to the outcome we observe empirically in ecological systems. A few species have lots of members and most species have very few, which is exactly what we see with corporate forms. A plausible hypothesis is that, in any given system, rare species are rare because, for whatever reason, they have not adapted well to their environment. Similarly, abundant species must have particular attributes which enable them to flourish. But the word 'neutral' in this context means that *no* species has any special qualities or characteristics which make it more or less suitable to operate in its given environment. Their relative success or failure is 'neutral' to their attributes. In other words, how a species behaves, what it can and cannot do, is irrelevant to whether or not at any point in time its numbers are small or large. The outcomes which we observe are the result of purely random processes.

It is a disturbing theory, which appears to defy common sense. But common sense tells us that it is the Sun which goes round the Earth and not vice versa. We see the Sun move, but we seem to stay still. However, like heliocentrism, neutral theory has the great strength that it fits the facts. Yes, evolution takes place, but the eventual outcome and the eventual 'winner' are determined much more at random than by inherent fitness. The policy implications of this are important. If we think the neutral theory applies in any serious way to corporate structures, and if we wish to at least challenge the dominance of the shareholder company we must allow more innovation, to allow different forms to come forward, one of which will eventually replace the dominant species.

Theories of Evolving Systems

In this book we draw heavily on recent advances in theory. In fact, our thesis is not only supported by this new theory; rather it might be preferable to say that our thesis emerges from it. Here we will briefly explain what this theoretical material is. We are mainly drawing from a body of literature which is best labelled *the complexity sciences*. This broad domain looks at interconnected, dynamic systems that are collectively known in the academic literature as *complex systems*. Such systems are made up of potentially large numbers of constituent parts (or 'agents') that interact with each other and adapt to each other over time. These systems *evolve*. Indeed, evolution is a running theme throughout this book and we also draw from related subjects like evolutionary economics.

In order to make this book accessible to a wide audience we will be careful to express our arguments and analysis in a non-technical way. For example, rather than refer to the confusing term 'complex systems', we instead emphasise *dynamic networks*, which are easier to visualise. But we mean the same thing.

The Over-Arching Thesis

The economic process is fundamentally an evolutionary one. Moreover, evolution within human systems is much more rapid than in the natural world where variation occurs between generations as a result of genetic change. In natural selection, this process is inter-generational and can span eons. By comparison, human cognitive processes are such that we can change some of the DNA of our societies *intra*-generationally – at times very rapidly – which includes laws pertaining to economic behaviour and institutions.

It gets much more complicated than this because not only do organisations adapt to their own changing environments, they adapt to each other too, simultaneously. This is known as *co-evolution*. Furthermore, the technological and legislative environments co-evolve too. Technology changes, organisations adapt – including through further innovation – causing others to adapt, leading to change that cascades across the whole economic system. But, as we saw above in the case of the industrial revolution, changes in legislation were required to cope with the challenges thrown up by new technology (noticeably in the form of the Joint Stock Companies Acts of 1844 and 1856). And, even further, these changes led to changes within organisations and industries, including the 'Great Consolidation' mergers and acquisitions phase of the early 20th Century.

At the risk of painting an ever more intractable picture of the economic process, economic theory has also been an integral part of this co-evolving process. Consistent with economic historians, we identify two broad epochs at work during the past few hundred years, incorporating two counterpart paradigms within economics. In addition, we posit that a third epoch with a third economics paradigm is emerging today centred around the stunning impact of ICT on the world economy. Consistent with the preceding section, the new paradigm emerging in economics is referred to here as the study of *dynamic networks*. This new paradigm lies at the heart of this thesis and, we argue, it has important implications for legislation concerned with organisational forms.

The first epoch can be referred to as the *mercantilist period* and was orientated around sovereign power. There is no clearly defined strand of mercantilist literature because economics was still discussed in the context of the wider political economy. However, we can say that mercantilism led to policies such as protectionism, export subsidies, and the accumulation of foreign exchange reserves by running a balance of payments surplus. In addition, the royal family and successive British governments exercised a tight control over some corporations, which until 1825 could only be incorporated by an act of parliament or by Royal Charter.

Many corporations during the mercantilist period were also co-owned by private individuals and the government/ the Crown. In addition, many corporations were given formidable powers, the most obvious example being the British East India Company, which was granted a Royal Charter in 1600 and which at one point had its own private army. It is not unreasonable to say that the mercantilist approach to economics both influenced *and was influenced by* the policies of the government at the time i.e. theory and practice co-evolved. The second epoch can be firmly associated with Adam Smith's great work, *The Wealth of Nations*, which was published in 1776. This book can be viewed as a demarcation between the earlier mercantilist period and the next paradigm in economics. *Classical economics* was born, emphasising the power of economic autonomy, the invisible hand, and the incentivising effect of free markets.

In a very real sense, the Joint Stock Companies Acts of 1844 and 1856 can be viewed as a manifestation of classical economics and the demise of mercantilism. These acts helped to reduce the influence of the government and the Crown on private individuals because the process of incorporation became more rule-based and was less at the whim of political discretion. To the extent that 'root causes' can be identified in dynamic, co-evolving systems, we can

24

see that classical economics, and the policies that followed, emerged out of the European Enlightenment of the 18th century. This was a much broader social and academic revolution that catalysed a broad-based shift of power from the church, government and monarch to private individuals and corporations. The Joint Stock Companies Acts of 1844 and 1856 ought to be viewed in this wider context.

We believe a third epoch is emerging today, which involves new ICT catalysing a rapidly changing environment for most organisations. At the same time, new economic theory has emerged out of this same technology – the processing power of computers – which is befitting of the new dynamic and networked economy. That is the study of dynamic networks. Networked computers have transformed how business is operating and the economy is now evolving rapidly. This change looks to be as significant as the industrial revolution itself and it demands that we look afresh at the legislation on which organisations are based. This is a key motivation for writing this book. Indeed, in order to illustrate what we mean by the need for new legislation, in Chapter 6 we take a closer look at the new, emerging economy and propose that a new organisational form is created – the for-benefit corporation – to hold and protect common assets.

But we want to take a further step back and question not only the specific legislation pertaining to organisations in the UK. We also want to question the *process* through which such legislation is arrived at. Specifically, we will argue that because the economic system is fundamentally evolutionary in nature, we need a legislative process that allows new forms of organisations to emerge and evolve over time (as mentioned above, we view these as equivalent to new species). In one sense, statutory law concerned with organisations needs to look more like common law: influenced by ground-up emergent processes and evolving over time as society changes. It needs to become both more democratic and dynamic and, as we argue in this book, its prime role is to reduce the uncertainty faced by stakeholders involved with organisations.

2

Organisations

Having outlined the main thesis of this book in the last chapter, here we will take a step back to build up a picture of organisations in the wider economy. This will help us build the foundations of our policy recommendations later in the book. The economic picture we build is one of a creative, evolving network of interacting parts in which organisations are essential. This chapter looks at the 'real' motivations for forming organisations: why do people group together at all in the economy? In the next chapter we will look at the history of the types of legal forms that have emerged in Britain over the past few hundred years. In this chapter we focus exclusively on why organisations exist at all, regardless of the law.

We want to do this from a standpoint of the new, emerging paradigm in economics and management science (a part of the third epoch referred to above), rather than the traditional perspective of mainstream economics (the second epoch). There are some important differences between these two, which matter for how we think of the legislative environment in which organisations operate. For example, the new paradigm informs us that we should not expect to 'solve' the problem of corporate law once and for all. The economy will always evolve and we should expect organisations and organisation law to change and to co-evolve over time. This is a continuous challenge.

To proceed, we must begin from the messy, intractable real world and work 'upwards' in order to develop a conceptual framework. This approach is motivated by an important principle in the new paradigm of dynamic systems: that these systems are constantly evolving. Over a long enough time horizon, behaviour and values change, which means we need to be constantly re-assessing how the economy works. That said, there are some 'deep patterns' of behaviour that we can usefully recognise and articulate. For example, and most importantly for this chapter, we argue that organisations exist for two fundamental reasons (at least):

(i) to exploit the combination of *specialisation* and *integration*[1] *among specialists*; and

(ii) to provide a platform which enables creativity.

These characteristics of organisations have existed for a very long time and we think it is reasonable to expect that this will remain true for a long time to come. They are deep patterns that we recognise and can relate to in our organisational lives. Indeed, these two rationales are related to the important concepts of *efficiency* and *resilience*[2] in ecosystems. Biological ecosystems may seem remote from the world of human economic activity and organisations, however there are some close parallels. For instance, both are systems in which the component parts interact with each other i.e. they are both dynamic networks. Moreover, there are many empirical similarities, including the mathematical relationships which describe the frequency with which 'extinction events' occur. We noted this in Chapter 1.

By organising themselves in a way that combines specialists and techniques for integrating these specialists, organisations can achieve an efficiency that allows them to survive in their environment today. But efficiency needs to be combined with the ability to adapt appropriately as the environment changes. Organisations do this by being creative – using ingenuity – in order to cope with an evolving economy. So, crudely put, the two features of organisations highlighted above correlate with the two notions of efficiency and resilience, respectively.

In the next section we ask the 'micro' – or 'ground-up' – question of why organisations exist at all. We will look at the standard neoclassical view and contrast this with a new paradigm perspective, which itself emerges out of a view of human nature and interaction that is more realistic than the neoclassical perspective. From these ground-up origins we can build up the picture of an economic system as a network of organisations, which are themselves dynamic networks of interacting people. In the next chapter we will look at how different organisational laws have emerged in the UK, and Chapter 4 will discuss how organisational law does and ought to relate to the economic system.

To some readers it might seem unnecessary to build up a picture of the economy as a dynamic network because this is self-evident. We think, however, that this is a useful exercise for two reasons. First, the neoclassical view of economics is so deeply embedded in how we make sense of the economy that we need to articulate a different and more realistic framing of the economic process. Second, in so doing we lay the foundations for our arguments in later chapters.

Why Do Organisations Exist? And What Are They?

Answering these questions will help us build a realistic understanding of what organisations are. They are, after all, a key building block of today's economy. It will also highlight the gaps in mainstream economics, which will be useful because public policies concerned with organisations, including the law, are informed by a paradigm that is insufficient for describing today's world. In effect, and speaking in broad terms, the older epoch describes the industrial economy of the 19th Century and not the integrated, dynamic economy of the 21st Century.

In building these foundations, we will delve briefly into some literature that is very compatible with the new economic paradigm, including *Organisation Theory, the Management Sciences,* and the work of Mark Granovetter, a sociologist.

The Neoclassical View

According to the old economics paradigm, organisations exist to minimise the transaction costs between people working in organisations. This view is attributed to Ronald Coase and Oliver Williamson, both of whom received the Nobel Memorial Prize in Economics for their work. What this means is that people working in a company need only to agree one contract, with the company itself, which includes the terms of their employment, rather than a potentially large number of bilateral agreements with all other employees. So, for example, if an organisation had 100 employees, each might require 99 contracts i.e. one with each other employee, or 9,900 bilateral contracts. However, if the organisation had a separate individual legal identity, then only 100 contracts are required, or one for each employee. The implication is that if such transaction costs did not exist, the world would be much more like the neoclassical world, which contains only individual agents and no firms. This view, however, emerges from the particular approach to economics taken by the classical and neoclassical schools. A thorough critique of these schools is beyond the scope of this book but it is worth mentioning a few key points.

From the point of view of the dynamic networks literature, we will highlight two problems with the neoclassical school: how it views individuals, and how it views the whole system. Individuals are viewed *as if* they had more sophisticated computational skills than they have in reality. We will see later on that this matters because it is our real cognitive limitations that lead us to specialise. In addition, the neoclassical school uses a radically simplistic view of *interaction*, namely that people engage in bilateral exchange which they can opt out of. In the conventional approach there is also indirect interaction via markets (all agents influence market prices, which in turn influence all agents). But, in general terms, the whole system is a group of automatons interacting mechanistically, like cogs in a machine. Some would refer to this broad approach as the *ontology of the neoclassical school*, whereas others would refer to the neoclassical *framing* of the subject. However put, the neoclassical school is in essence a collection of specific premises on which neoclassical models are then built and policy makers then advised.

Given this framework, if we add transaction costs to the mix we can see where the neoclassical view of why firms exist comes from, which is to minimise internal transaction costs. By allowing firms to take on the legal identity of an individual, employees need only have one contract. Importantly, we are not saying that this explanation for the existence of the firm is necessarily wrong. It is internally coherent. However, such models are not necessarily reflective of the real world, however coherent they are internally. Recall our example of the sun moving around a static earth in the opening chapter. We would also emphasise a point made above, that mainstream economics does a good job of describing the economy of the 19th Century. In the 21st Century economy, this rationale of minimising transaction costs is left wanting and we feel it is necessary to find a better and more realistic explanation for why organisations exist before proceeding.

It may seem that we are being pedantic in critiquing the neoclassical approach to firms. Theories are after all well known to be approximations of reality. We would offer three points in response. First, some theories are less inaccurate than others, and we think it preferable to use the least inaccurate ones. Second, we think it is *self-evident* that we ought to build up a robust understanding of why organisations exist, which we can all relate to in our everyday lives. And, third, the institutions and laws (including corporate law) on which the UK's economy is built are founded on this same neoclassical ontology, so this highly abstract and inaccurate approach is actually endemic. We will return to this point later but, as should be clear by now, a theme of this book is that we now have the conceptual technology to move beyond neoclassical economics.

New Paradigm Approaches

We have referred several times to the new emerging paradigm in economics, orientated around dynamic networks. The management sciences also seem to be undergoing an equivalent paradigm change, which is due to our improved understanding of networks. Here we will use this new approach to flesh out a much more robust and realistic view of why organisations exist at all. Fortunately, this question has been thought about a great deal already in *Organisation Theory*, so we need not start from scratch. The particular strands of Organisation Theory we refer to below sit comfortably with the emerging paradigm in economics.

As we know, in reality we are cognitively and physically limited and we are also influenced by psychological factors. Moreover, we can all understand that our personalities and identities have emerged from a combination of inherited biology and our historical experiences, including education and training. The concept of path dependence applies to who we are today because we have emerged in part from the influences on us through our lives. Two of the most insightful thinkers in this area are Herbert Simon and Daniel Kahneman. Simon's work on the limits to human cognition was substantial and included the now well-known concept of *bounded rationality*. This includes the idea that we have cognitive limits to the information we can process and limited time for processing it. Kahneman's work in differentiating between System 1 cognition ('quick thinking') and System 2 cognition ('slow thinking') is also helpful. System 1 thinking is related to the idea of pattern recognition, and is consistent with skills training through repetition. Over a period of time, the human brain becomes familiar with repeated patterns of behaviour, and this can develop in to what we commonly refer to as *expertise*.

These real constraints, those that truly limit how we work in an economy, lead many of us to *specialise* in particular professions, tradecrafts, or skilled work. Focus of attention and repetition over time breed specialised skills, and by specialising we are able to become more productive. The efficiency gains from specialisation are well understood. For example, Adam Smith famously referred to the rise in productivity in pin manufacturing due to people specialising:

> One man draws out the wire, another straightens it, a third cuts it, and a fourth points it, a fifth grinds it at the top for receiving the head; to make the head requires two or three distinct operations; to put it on is a percularia business, the whiten the pin is another; it is even a trade by itself to put them in to the book; and the important business of making a pin is, in this manner, divided into about eighteen distinct operations.[3]

Moreover, human interaction is much more sophisticated and subtle than that implied by neoclassical economics. We communicate on multiple levels (including body language and audible language) for a variety of reasons. In addition, very often we become engaged in repeated interactions, relationship formation, power plays, inter-personal politics, and so forth. There is a substantial literature in this domain, for example, Gregory Bateson's *An Ecology of the Mind* and Norbert Elias' *The Civilizing Process.*

Organisation Theory

Our emphasis on the combination of specialisation and integration, while different from the focus of the neoclassical school, is a point emphasised in Organisation Theory. In fact, in a book of the same name, Mary Jo Hatch noted that while there are multiple approaches and theories within Organisation Theory, there is a general consensus that this combination of specialisation and integration is why organisations exist at all. Note, for example, this extract from *Organization Theory*:

Social Structure As Differentiation And Integration

Organization Theorists often claim that organisations form around tasks that are too large for individuals to perform by themselves. The advantage of organizations over individuals, they explain, comes from pooling different skills and abilities. If some persons take responsibility for one part of a task, while others perform other parts, much can be achieved that would be impossible otherwise. Consider the example of NASA. No one individual would have been capable of a moon landing. This extraordinary achievement was accomplished through the organized efforts not only of scientists, engineers, and astronauts, but also technicians, production workers, maintenance workers, clerical employees, and mangers (not to mention organised efforts within the scientific community, the defence industry, and the United States government). Of course, the advantages of organization can be lost if differentiated tasks and workers are not well integrated, as the NASA Challenger disaster of 1986 so painfully made clear.[4]

We would agree with this consensus view, which sits comfortably with the emerging paradigm in economics. The reason for the difference between Organisation Theory and neo-classicists is that the premises contained in the latter, namely its assumptions regarding human cognition and interaction, do not constrain the former in the same way. This is also true of dynamic network approaches, which, as stated, build up a conceptual framework from the real world, unburdened by inherited assumptions that 'make the maths easier'.

An example of research within Organisation Theory focused on specialisation and integration is the work of James Thompson.[5] Thompson looked at how work may be interrelated, such that changes in one part of an organisation's network influence other parts of that network. The tasks of certain specialists might be inter-dependent, which requires coordination. Thompson differentiated between three different types of co-ordination. The first he called *pooled task interdependence*, which is when the nature of requisite co-ordination is simple and only involves things such as rules and standard operating procedures which mechanistically co-ordinate the actions of different people. For example, day and night shifts on an assembly line can be co-ordinated via simple written procedures. The second type of co-ordination results from what Thompson called *sequential task interdependence*. The most obvious example of this is an assembly line where one person's work will be contingent on those operating 'earlier' in the production line. If one worker is not performing their task correctly, they will affect those further down the line. Co-ordination required with this type of inter-dependence includes planning and scheduling.

A more sophisticated type, which is Thompson's third category, is *reciprocal task interdependence*. This is where people working in an organisation have to co-ordinate in real-time, or near real-time. For example, in a restaurant, the waiting staff and kitchen staff are dependent on each other: the kitchen staff on the waiters for orders, and the waiters on the kitchen staff to make the food. The co-ordination between such interdependent tasks is much more sophisticated than for the other two types, and typically requires pre-agreed roles and tasks in addition to mutual adjustment when required. We might simply call this *teamwork*. Thompson's work is a good example of the literature within Organisation Theory which focuses on the need to co-ordinate, or integrate, specialised work within organisations.

Specialisation and Integration

We would characterise the relationship between specialisation and integration as *dialectical*, which is to say that within organisations one cannot exist successfully without the other. This should be obvious. A collection of specialised individuals (let's say in an oil production company) acting without any form of integration couldn't possibly operate successfully. Oil drilling needs to be co-ordinated very carefully, ensuring a smooth flow of oil from well to refinery in a way that means no or few resources are left idle; that stocks do not exceed capacity constraints; and that this is all done safely.

Equivalently, an organisation that only collaborates and has nobody specialising is unlikely to be as successful as it could be. This is something of an over-generalisation of course – organisations operating in highly changeable environments may prefer to employ only generalists who can adapt quickly. But, on the whole, organisations employ specialists, including sales people, managers, accountants etc. whose actions must be integrated for the organisation to be effective. Put another way, as specialisation increases within organisations, the greater there will be a need to integrate, or co-ordinate, the various functions. Paradoxically, therefore, specialisation leads to greater contingency within a network, which leads to a greater need for interaction to achieve integration.

So far in this chapter we have referred mainly to specialisation among skilled workers but we can also think of physical resources and technology as forms of specialisation. The most obvious example is a computer, which performs functions that human beings cannot (which is also true vice versa). Similarly, when we speak about integration, we are not only referring to people co-ordinating their actions through conversation. Integration can also involve management processes (which can also be viewed as a form of technology), behaviour protocols, systems and controls, task schedules, standard operating procedures, etc. So specialisation and integration are about more than just human processes and interaction.

Furthermore, it is worthwhile noting that this dialectical relationship between specialisation and integration should not be viewed as a static process. It is inherently dynamic because specialist skills and integration co-evolve together as well as with other factors, including technological change.

Specialisation and Uncertainty

The productivity gains that result from specialisation are well understood. Here we note briefly that there is a relationship between specialisation and uncertainty, which links to an argument we make later in the book about the role of the law in mitigating uncertainty. In highly volatile, uncertain environments, investing in training to develop people's specialised skills is risky both for an organisation and for individuals. If the environment changes then any training might become obsolete. A higher degree of certainty about the environment in which an organisation is operating will reduce this risk. A reduced level of uncertainty, therefore, is likely to encourage investments in specialised skills (by both individuals and employers), thereby enhancing productivity. A general policy conclusion we draw from this is that an aim of government ought to be to mitigate (it cannot eliminate) the uncertainty faced by organisations. One way in which it can do this is to ensure the statutory law concerned with organisations reduces as far as practicable the uncertainty that they face. We discuss this further in chapters 3 and 4.

Platforms to Enable Creativity

Here we flesh out the second main rationale for organisations, that they are platforms enabling creativity within the economy. This second rationale is linked to an important part of this book, namely the inherently dynamic nature of organisations and the economy. To understand this point in more detail, we can once again draw on the new paradigm of dynamic networks. Some argue that the most important feature of this new approach is the concept of *emergence* because it takes us out of the machine-like mind-set which has dominated Western academia since the Enlightenment, including neoclassical economics. A detailed discussion of this point is beyond the scope of this book, however Stuart Kauffman's *Re-Inventing the Sacred* is a useful reference.

The essential point for this book is that the future of economic systems, including the environments in which organisations have to operate, is *inherently indeterminable* due to emergent properties. This represents a crucial difference between neoclassical economics and a dynamic networks approach, and it helps us to understand that a major challenge for organisations is to be robust in the face of events that cannot be determined ahead of time. To the managers of most organisations, this point will be empirically obvious. However, it is missing from the ontology of the neoclassical school, which focuses on economic efficiency and not resilience. Organisations, therefore, have to adapt in the moment to uncertain events as they arise, and to do this they need to be creative. The second rationale for the existence of organisations is therefore to provide a platform for its employees to adapt, i.e. react creatively, in the face of unforeseen events.

A great deal of work has been done looking at creativity within organisations in the Management Sciences literature. Most notable is the work of Peter Allen, now an Emeritus Professor at the Cranfield School of Management.[6] Allen's work demonstrated that groups of people (including organisations) are most creative when people with different skills and perspectives are brought together. For example, a Board of Directors made up of CEO clones is unlikely to be very creative. Allen's work has emphasised that the combination of diverse points of view is an essential ingredient in the creative process. If we return to our emphasis on the economic process as being an inherently evolutionary one, we can see that creativity plays a role similar to that of genetic variation in natural selection. There is an important difference, however, because genetic variation is random in nature whereas creativity in organisations is purposeful, at least most of the time.

Moreover, while enabling creativity in the face of unpredictable events is important, it is worth noting that *one organisation's adaptation is another's environmental change.* For example, if one firm's supplier innovates in some way, that may have implications for the firm, which itself might adapt. With this picture in mind, we can see that the economy is a network in a state of perpetual change, involving people in organisations reacting creatively to each other.

The Economy as a Network of Interacting Networks

Until now this chapter has focused on why organisations exist, moving away from the standard neoclassical view of minimising transaction costs to one which emphasises specialisation with integration, and creativity. As should be obvious, organisations are *the* base unit of today's economy. But we should not think of organisations as *closed systems.* They are *open systems* in the sense that they interact with other organisations in many direct and indirect ways. They are also open to flows of information and energy. In this book we would offer the idea that the economy ought to be viewed as a network of open networked systems. In framing the economy in this way, we begin to understand why it is important and useful to tap into the growing literature concerned with dynamic networks. The economy *is* a dynamic network and it is preferable to think of it like that as opposed to the static framing of mainstream economics. Taking this approach leads to realise important implications for any legislation concerned with organisations, which we will come on to.

The economy is not *only* a network of interacting people and organisations. It is also subject to patterns of behaviour, including norms, values, and the law, and many of these are culture-specific. Interestingly, while we have reached this conclusion through the new sciences of dynamic networks, it relates closely to the work of certain sociologists, notably Mark Granovetter and his notion of 'embeddedness'. This is the idea that economic behaviour and institutions are constrained by on-going social relations, such that it would be wrong to consider economic actions as independent of wider cultural traits.

The Implications for Legislation

In the next chapter we switch our focus to looking at various forms of organisation and how these emerged over time in the UK. But before we do that, we will propose a general principle that any law pertaining to organisations ought to take in to account.

A number of researchers concerned with dynamic networks discuss the *enabling and constraining environment* in which the constituents of the system (agents) operate. The law – including statutory and common law – is an important part of this environment. We have argued in this chapter that there are two related core rationales for the existence of organisations: to benefit from the efficiency gains arising from integrating specialised functions; and to benefit from the creativity potential of people operating together. If this is the case, then any legislation relating to organisations should *enable* both of these things, and, in addition, it should seek to remove any inappropriate *constraints* on them.

3

The Emergence of Different Organisational Forms

Chapter 1 of this book set out the argument that the economic process is fundamentally an evolutionary one. It is not the static process described, broadly speaking, by mainstream economics. Chapter 2 added further colour to this framing in describing the economy as a dynamic, integrated network of organisations, which themselves ought to be thought of as dynamic networks. They leverage the efficiency gains arising from specialisation and integration, and provide platforms to enable creativity.

In this chapter we will look at some of the *legal history* that is relevant to the organisational forms we see today in the UK, focusing in particular on the Joint Stock Company, which is by far the most prevalent type of legal entity across much of the Western world. This history will reinforce the idea that the economy is a dynamic, evolutionary process; and it will help to contextualise the organisational forms we see about us today (see Appendix 1). In this chapter we will look at partnerships, joint stock companies, industrial and provident societies, co-operatives, charities, and community interest companies.

In chapter 4 we develop a much broader discussion of the issues relating to the law concerned with organisational forms. Chapter 5 focuses specifically on the Joint Stock Company. Before proceeding, it is important to acknowledge that the law relating to organisations is vast; and that in this book we concern ourselves mostly, but not exclusively, with *statutory law* i.e. that which is written by Parliament. There are two other main categories of law that we will also mention, including *common law*, which is based on case law and precedent; and *regulatory law*, which relates to the agencies of government (such as the Charity Commission). Moreover, this chapter seeks only to draw out some important parts of the relevant history, in addition to points pertinent to this book. It is not meant as an exhaustive survey.

Partnerships

We begin with partnership law, which is the oldest form of law relating to organisations in England, preceding statutory law concerned with joint stock companies by several hundred years. Indeed, partnership law was largely a matter of common law until 1865 when the first statutory partnership law was passed. In the period of globalised markets, multinational companies and rapid information flows, it is easy to lose sight of the fact that our economy emerged from the humble, local level, involving small numbers of people grouping together to form partnerships. In such circumstances, it was natural for common law to be the main legal form applied to organisations.

Although it emerged mostly from the indigenous national economy, other countries also influenced those aspects of the UK's common law concerning partnerships. For example, around the 15th Century, Italian merchants brought to Great Britain and other parts of northern Europe a number of the foundations of the law relating to banking and commercial partnerships. It is not unusual in the history of law for such legal innovations and concepts to be copied from other domains. Within Europe, there were two broad types of partnership by the 17th Century. The first, favoured in France, was known as the *Commenda* and was a form of limited partnership. It allowed wealthy people to invest in partnerships in return for a share of the profit. This type of partnership avoided usury laws and was also structured so that the liability of each investor was limited to their share in the partnership (an early form of limited liability). This form of partnership, however, did not find favour in England until 2000.

The second type of partnership was the *Societas*, which is a form of normal (or 'ordinary') partnership in which all of the partners were held responsible for the debts of the company. This form of partnership *was* emphasised in England. Indeed, by the 17th Century, common law relating to partnerships contained two of the key principles of normal partnerships that still exist today: that when two or more people are engaged in an unincorporated joint business venture, it is viewed as a partnership under the eyes of the law; and all of the partners are exposed to unlimited liability with respect to the obligations of the business. Importantly, the patchwork system of common law that existed in the early stages of the industrial revolution was seen as frustrating economic progress. For example, the Commissioners for Trade reported to the House of Commons in 1691 that the machinery for deciding 'controversies between merchants concerning accounts' was inadequate.[1] Similarly, Daniel Defoe argued at the end of the 17th Century for a new 'court merchant' to intermediate in disputes between merchants and tradesmen.[2] Despite these frustrations, the law concerning partnerships remained a matter for common law until 1865.

This insufficiency of common law highlighted an important issue with respect to the role of common and statutory law in the economy. Common law, which is admirable in its capacity to evolve over time as society changes and in its capacity to accommodate idiosyncrasies, is *in effect* backward looking. We will argue later in this book that an important rationale for statutory law within a dynamic, creative economy is to ensure the law is relevant to the *contemporaneous* conditions of the economy. This is in order to mitigate the uncertainty faced by people who own and work within organisations. In a sense, common law could be viewed as a *conservative* form of law i.e. it tends to change slowly and only in light of evidence for a need to change, whereas statutory law needs to be *progressive* i.e. contemporaneous and, if possible, forward-looking. We discuss this further in the next chapter.

Parliament organised its first statutory legislation concerning partnerships in the second half of the 19th Century, which was an important period of time for all statutory law concerned with organisations. It passed *The Law of Partnership Act* in 1865. However, this act was fairly limited in scope and was superseded by the Partnership Act of 1890. A key role of this latter act was to clarify and codify much of the common law that existed by 1890. This was important because it helped to reduce the uncertainty concerning partnership law in general, and, more specifically, it helped people who were not experts in the law to understand it better, including partners working in partnerships.

The Limited Partnerships Act 1907 helped to introduce the idea of a *limited partner*, which was concerned with partners not directly involved in the business and whose liability could be limited to their initial investment. Apart from this modification to partnership law, the 1890 Act formed the basis of partnership law for the next 110 years. The next major piece of partnership legislation was the Limited Liability Partnership Act of 2000. As suggested by the name, the main feature of this act was the creation of the Limited Liability Partnership (LLP).

Following the 2000 Act, today there are now three main types of partnerships in existence: normal partnerships, limited partnerships, and LLPs. An LLP is a new form of incorporation i.e. the act conferred on these businesses a separate legal identity, in addition to limited liability, in the same way that the Companies Act does. Moreover, partners in LLPs are not 'jointly and severally liable' for the actions of other members, which is still the case with normal partnerships. LLPs, therefore, look a lot like joint stock companies.

The Joint Stock Company

While the latter part of the 19th Century saw important acts of parliament agreed concerning partnerships – notably the Act of 1890 – by far the most important innovations in statutory law concerning organisations were the Joint Stock Companies Acts of 1844 and 1856 and the Limited Liability Act of 1855.

Together these acts laid down the two pillars that characterise modern companies today:

(i) a legal identity separate to its owners ('incorporation'); and
(ii) that a shareholder's liability was limited to his or her initial investment ('limited liability').

Ever since the South Sea Bubble of the early 18th Century, and the subsequent 'Bubble Act', ordinary people were prohibited from incorporating a joint stock company without an act of parliament or a royal charter. This prohibition was removed in 1825 and was subsequently clarified and codified by the acts of 1844 and 1856. These acts meant that any political discretion involved in incorporation was removed and incorporation became an administrative process much like we see today. The second characteristic of companies today – limited liability – was profoundly important and was a significant differentiator from normal partnerships in which, as mentioned above, partners were exposed to unlimited liability.

It is important to emphasise that neither of these two concepts were particularly new when the three acts mentioned above were passed by parliament. Both incorporation and limited liability had histories dating back several hundred years. For example, 'incorporation' has its legal roots in Roman law, and its etymological roots in Latin, from the word 'corpus', meaning 'body'. The Roman Empire saw the emergence of many organisational 'bodies' which were held to have distinct legal identities under the eyes of the law. Moreover, partnerships that included limited liability (the *Commenda* mentioned above) were prevalent on the continent for several hundred years. What was new in the three acts of parliament was the 'mobilisation' of the two concepts of incorporation and limited liability under statutory law in a way that made clear the rights and responsibilities of particular stakeholders involved in joint stock companies.

The Economics and Politics of the New Legislation

These historical facts, and the processes that led to the various acts of parliament, ought not to be viewed as merely political. They were in fact symptomatic of the profound shift underway in the economy, namely, the industrial revolution. It is probably more appropriate to say that these acts *emerged* from a broad *political economic process*. But that is not all: the statutory law that emerged also did so because common law was insufficient to handle the uncertainties that arose from the changing economy.

The shift from a broadly agrarian-based economy to an industrial one required large capital outlays, both in terms of industrial plants and infrastructure. Moreover, such economic change was unprecedented. The industrial revolution in Europe was the first of its kind in the world. This meant that the economic environment was even less certain than it is for today's emerging economies, which benefit from the large-scale demand provided by the global economy and also mature laws in industrial countries which they might copy or mimic. The industrialists of Europe's industrial revolution were in effect exploring the frontier of a new type of economy at a time of great technological change, and this involved a substantial amount of uncertainty. In Chapter 6 we argue that the world is in an equivalent period of change today due to ICT.

Before the acts of parliament of 1844, 1855 and 1856, most businesses were in the form of normal partnerships, which meant that partners were liable for the debts of the business. As technology increasingly enabled large-scale industrial production, the need to invest substantial sums in new businesses clashed with the unlimited liability feature of normal partnerships. Business owners and the providers of loan capital were being required to invest increasing sums of money in the new economy. This also involved potentially larger liabilities for which partners would be held personally responsible. These acts of parliament were important for mitigating the risk to people who wanted to own a business in the new economy and lenders who wanted to invest in those businesses. Put another way, the three acts of parliament and, more specifically, the characteristics of incorporation and limited liability helped to reduce investment uncertainty, thereby enabling substantial investments in large capital projects which were a part of and enabled the industrial revolution.

Given these comments about limited liability and incorporation, it is important that we not take these points too far. The acts of 1844, 1855 and 1856 were not agreed at the beginning of the industrial revolution, so it would be wrong to claim that these acts were wholly necessary for industrialisation. We merely claim here that these acts manifested from the need for such changes, given the changes afoot in the economy, and also they helped to further catalyse a process that was already under way. Moreover, we must also emphasise that we are not claiming that stock exchanges intermediated all capital investment after these acts of parliament. In fact there is a lot of evidence to suggest that reinvested profit remained an important source of capital for many firms after these acts of parliament. For example, in the Yorkshire woollen industry during much of the industrial revolution:

> External supplies of capital… were less important than the personal or family sums which the industrialists scraped together and ventured in the new productive equipment.[3]

It would be more appropriate to say that these three acts of parliament helped to channel investment funds into larger projects such as infrastructure outlays e.g. ports and railways; they enabled entrepreneurs with new investment ideas to seek funding from people they did not know; and they helped enable the great consolidation of the late 19th and early 20th century, which was described in the introduction to this book.

There is, of course, a legitimate question of whether limited liability – which has benefited industrialists and investors – involves costs for anybody else. Clearly, it can do because of the potential for fraud and also because of what are now referred to as *negative externalities* by economists. This is when a person or a firm has a negative impact on other parts of the economy without any agreed compensation (we use this as our working definition of externalities – it is slightly broader than what economists typically use). For example, if a corporation were to become insolvent, a number of stakeholders in the business are likely to suffer, including creditors, employees and suppliers. In these circumstances shareholders have no liability towards these other stakeholders over and above the net worth of the company, which means some stakeholders risk ending up out of pocket.

As a result of these potential negative externalities, corporations were required to make public certain information relating to their creditworthiness. In addition, companies had to adopt the suffix of 'Publicly Limited Company' (PLC) or, after 1907, 'Limited Liability' (LTD) to demonstrate to would-be stakeholders the risk they were undertaking. When added to the legal concept of *caveat emptor* ('buyer beware'), these two features mitigated – and continue to mitigate today – the potential risks to stakeholders of engaging with PLC and LTD corporations. It is important to emphasise, however, that these steps only mitigate the potential damage caused by limited liability. They are not fully preventative because they do not eliminate uncertainty. Moreover, when the benefits to risky behaviour exceed the potential costs, there is always a question of moral hazard to consider i.e. does the implicit insurance provided by limited liability cause the corporation to take greater risks? We consider this further in Chapter 5.

Also underway during the 19th Century, which we mentioned in the opening chapter, was a broad paradigm shift in economics from mercantilist thinking to what we now refer to as classical economics. This field was noted for its emphasis on individualism, free markets, and an increasing focus on analysing 'the firm', from which, in the early 20th century, emerged the 'theory of the firm'. The distinction between individuals and corporations was of course not new but classical theory helped to set the theoretical *context* for the joint stock company acts.

However, rather than saying that theory necessarily gave rise to these three acts, we would instead say that the classical paradigm in economics was merely *conducive* to the type of corporation that emerged in the late 19th Century. The specific characteristics of the joint stock company (incorporation and limited liability) ought not to be viewed as an inevitable by-product of the theory. The theory of the firm said nothing about incorporation – it was merely a theory of production. Indeed, the paradigm in which this theory emerged would emphasise the potential problems arising from moral hazard due to limited liability, implicitly questioning (we would argue) its legitimacy as a useful economic idea. As mentioned above, it is perhaps preferable to say that the joint stock company acts emerged out of a *political economic process*. It should be clear that the combination of incorporation and limited liability were largely in the interests of the industrialists and high net worth people of the time, who would have been very supportive of these acts of parliament.

There are two final points worth emphasising in this sub-section. First, there is nothing inherently 'natural', nor inherently special, about joint stock companies. They have been radically successful as a species but they remain a human construct, one that emerged out of a political economic process. Second, and very importantly, the joint stock company acts were appropriate for the *industrial* revolution when the newly emerging economy required larger capital outlays than previously. As we argue in Chapter 6, a new type of economy is emerging today so it is essential that we ask whether the organisational forms we have today, and the associated common and statutory laws, are conducive to enabling (and/or not constraining) this new economy to flourish.

Tectonic shifts

It is probably not unreasonable to say that the impact of these acts of parliament on the business world, and the economy more generally, were staggering. Within a few decades, the dominant form of enterprise in Britain switched from being the normal partnership to the joint stock company. Moreover, the three acts of parliament mentioned above were in effect replicated in many other countries. As a species, the joint stock company spread rapidly.

The Joint Stock Company Today

Above we saw that the two defining characteristics of joint stock companies since the acts of 1844 and 1856 were incorporation and limited liability. Since these acts, various other characteristics of joint stock companies have been added in the form of requirements by various company acts. The latest act is the Companies Act of 2006, which defines three types of company: limited by guarantee, limited by shares (private) and limited by shares (public).[4] For the remainder of this book, when we refer to joint stock companies we generally mean companies limited by shares (public), which are also known as Public Limited Companies (PLCs). The requirements of these companies as outlined by the Companies Act and stock exchange rules are substantial, and relate to the rights and responsibilities of shareholders, directors, and the company in general.

Industrial and Provident Societies (IPSs)

IPSs trace their origins back to the friendly society sector, which was once a key part of people's lives, notably in the provision of insurance and savings-type services. However, a distinct form of organisation emerged from this sector that became known as an IPS and this led to the Industrial and Provident Societies Partnership Act of 1852. Prior to that, these societies were bound by the Friendly Societies Act of 1834 but the nature of these organisations began to sit awkwardly with the earlier act, which led to questions being raised about the legality of particular societies. The 1852 Act put the legality of IPSs beyond doubt, which we offer as another example of how statutory law can and should evolve with the times, in order to reduce uncertainty. The Act also clarified what types of activities societies could undertake to be consistent with the Act. Broadly speaking, they had to behave in the interests of the community.

Historically, IPSs have been used mainly as a form of *collective action* by groups of people with modest amounts of capital, to help with the provision of certain necessities. Notably, the 1852 Act referred specifically to the provision of 'food, lodging, clothing, and other necessities'. In understanding the background to IPSs it is important to appreciate that the welfare state did not exist in the 19th Century (it emerged in its current form after the Second World War); and neither was there a versatile, competitive economy of the type we see today. As a result, a number of goods and services were simply not provided by the state or the market in the earlier years of the industrial revolution. This often necessitated people acting collectively to ensure particular necessities were provided to them.

IPSs represent a different type of incorporation to the three types of company required to register with Companies House today i.e. Public Limited Companies, Companies Limited by Guarantee, and Companies Limited by Shares. The process of incorporation for IPSs relates to different statutory law. Today, IPSs have to be registered with the Financial Services Authority in a process that includes providing the registrar with a set of rules for the Society. Currently, the Registrar examines these rules to see whether they are in compliance with the Industrial and Provident Societies Act 1965.

Since the 1965 act, IPSs have been registered either as a co-operative or for the benefit of the community. The fact that some IPSs are co-operatives causes confusion, increased by the fact that co-operatives can also be incorporated under different statutes, including the Companies Act 2006. We try to clarify the typology of organisations in Appendix 1. One part of IPS history is worth dwelling on because it demonstrates the potential abuse of having different types of organisations in existence. During the 1930s, a number of IPSs sprang up offering property and share schemes: it appeared the main rationale was to help those offering the funds to avoid Companies Act prospectus requirements. This led to would-be investors being duped because of the mis-leading nature and general paucity of the information available. Many small investors suffered significant losses, which led to a national campaign to curtail the abuses. The result was a bill that led to IPSs being banned from engaging in investment business.

This history is mentioned to highlight a problem with having a wide variety of organisations under the auspices of multiple acts of parliament. In effect, the IPS legislation of the 1930s enabled unscrupulous people to engage in what amounted to 'organisation arbitrage' whereby an activity that ought to have been located in one type of organisation (such as those bound by the Companies Act) was placed in another. IPSs were and continue to be viewed as being for the benefit of the community so this 'brand' sits awkwardly with the real risk of investment funds. We further discuss the need to protect 'statutory brands' in the next chapter. Today, IPSs constitute a small part of the whole economy (see Appendix 1). Moreover, when the Cooperatives and Community Benefit Societies and Credit Unions Act 2010 comes in to force, IPSs will technically cease to exist. They will be split into three types: Co-operative Societies, Community Benefit Societies, and Pre-2010 Act societies.

Co-operatives

As should be clear by the name, co-operatives involve the application of co-operative principles to business organisations. The two main types of co-operative are customer-owned co-operatives (which includes the well know UK brand name, *The Co-Op*) and employee-owned co-operatives (*The John Lewis Partnership* and *Suma Wholefoods* are examples). The owners of the organisation are often referred to as *members*, in whose interests the organisation is managed. The history of co-operatives goes back several hundred years; however a key period in the history of this organisational form was the 19th Century, when the *co-operative movement* got going across Europe. In the UK this movement was both typified and catalysed by the Rochdale Society of Equitable Pioneers (aka *The Rochdale Pioneers*) when they articulated the *Rochdale Principles* in 1844.

The Rochdale Principles include:

(i)   Voluntary and open membership
(ii)   Democratic member control
(iii) Member economic participation
(iv) Autonomy and independence
(v)   Education, training, and information
(vi) Co-operation among co-operatives
(vii) Concern for community

These principles were subsequently taken up by the International Co-operative Alliance in 1937 (and subsequently updated), meaning that the co-operative movement took up these principles worldwide. A co-operative is, however, *not* a form of incorporation in much the same way that charities are not. Co-operatives can take one of several forms of incorporation, including the three types of companies registered with Companies House: an IPS, an LLP, or as a normal partnership. However, historically, the type of incorporation most associated with co-operatives was the IPS because of the close alignment between the values and principles of both i.e. the IPS was a natural form of incorporation for co-operatives.

The Cooperatives and Community Benefit Societies and Credit Unions Act 2010, mentioned above in relation to IPSs will, once it is brought in to force, provide a legal structure designed with co-operatives in mind. In recent years, co-operatives have found favour with the coalition government which came to power in 2010 because co-operatives appear broadly compatible with the government's Big Society agenda. That agenda seeks to enhance civil society, including forms of co-operative ownership and control. As a result, in January 2012 the government announced that it would make further changes to the legislation in order to simplify and clarify statutory law relating to co-operatives.

Charities

Statutory law concerned with charities dates back to the 16th and 17th centuries, notably the Charitable Uses Act of 1601 (otherwise known as the 'Statute of Elizabeth', after Queen Elizabeth I). The history of this Act is another example of statutory law emerging from a broadly political economic process. During the 16th Century, Britain was hit by several natural and man-made disasters, including outbreaks of plague, the Anglo-Spanish war that started in 1585, several disastrous harvests, and economic depression. At around the same time, the role of the church in charitable work declined. This combination led to large-scale deprivation across the country, moving the government and the monarch of the time, Elizabeth I, to do something about it.

One of their answers was the 1601 Act, which worked in conjunction with other acts of parliament (notably the 1601 Poor Law) to address the manifold social problems that were afflicting the country at that time. These acts in effect created a proxy for today's welfare state whereby the church was required to organise the delivery of care, education and employment services. They also helped to support and enable the charity sector, and it also imposed a governance structure on charities, which included bishops taking on the role of commissioners to supervise and administer charitable activities in their jurisdiction.

The government and the monarch were at the 'top' of this governance hierarchy. From the late 17th Century, charities were granted exemptions from land tax, and this exemption carried over to income tax when it was introduced in 1799. William Gladstone, when he was Chancellor of the Exchequer, fought against the exemption of charities in 1863 but he was defeated so the income tax exemption remained.

From this short history of statutory charity law, two key principles emerge:

(i) the role of the government in the governance of the charity sector;
(ii) tax exemption for charities.

Concerning the first principle, in the early days of charity law, the governance of the sector appeared more like an attempt to force the church to provide particular welfare services to those in need. Today, the rationale for the government being involved in the governance of charities appears to be one of collective action and resource pooling rather than control.

What economists call *information asymmetries* are more pronounced in the charity sector than for companies selling goods and services. When it comes to buying a car, for example, it is obvious what you are getting and whether the product is value for money. In the charity sector, most contributors (though certainly not all) spend no time on due diligence before giving, and no time assessing the impact of their donation. This opens charities up to abuse. Moreover, few charity contributors are likely to build an agency from scratch to provide supervision because of the free-rider problem. This establishes a rationale for the government to build an agency that supervises charities to ensure donations are being put to good effect. This is an example of both collective action and resource pooling.

The detailed intricacies of the tax exemptions granted to charities and charitable contributions need not concern us here but it should be obvious that if one group of organisations are given tax exemptions, the government will have to police such organisations. It is inevitable that some owners and managers of profit-seeking corporations, for example, will be tempted to claim charity status in order to benefit from the beneficial tax treatment charities receive. It is reasonable, therefore, that the government monitors charities to ensure they are not merely companies seeking to evade tax.

Today, charities are required to register as a charity with the Charity Commission; and they may take on various forms of incorporation, or they may be unincorporated. Furthermore, a new form of charity will soon be permitted, known as the Charitable Incorporated Organisation (CIO), which will have its own form of incorporation. These various points are explained in more detail in Appendix 1.

Community Interest Companies (CICs)

The newest form of organisation to have emerged in the UK is the CIC, with its counterpart statutory law having received royal ascent in October 2004. In a nutshell, the CIC emerged out of two things coming together. The first was a conversation between Stephen Lloyd, a lawyer specialising in Charity Law who works for Baites, Wells, and Braithwaite, and Roger Warren-Evans, an entrepreneur. This conversation led to Warren-Evans writing a pamphlet which promoted the idea of a 'Public Interest Company'.[5] This formed the basis of the subsequent CIC.

The second was a desire by the then Labour government to help foster and enable social enterprises. There was a general perception within government, notably within the Cabinet Office's Strategy Unit, that appropriate incorporation options were unavailable to people who wanted to manage organisations and contribute to their communities at the same time i.e. social entrepreneurs. The Strategy Unit's 2002 paper *Private Action, Public Benefit* noted that the social enterprise sector was growing fast but at the time the various forms of incorporation were largely unsuited. A new vehicle was needed, and the Strategy Unit took note of the pamphlet written by Lloyd and Warren-Evans. After consultations and deliberations, the CIC was born.

The process of creating a CIC is similar to that of forming a charity. A CIC has to be registered as a company with Companies House (in any of the three company forms) and must also register with the CIC Regulator. The Regulator's job is to ensure that the stated aims of each CIC are consistent with statute. A CIC must be a company – it cannot assume any other form of incorporation.

Two key features of CICs are the restrictions on the distribution of dividends, and an asset lock. Dividend distribution is limited because the purpose of a CIC is to run the organisation *in the interests of the community*. Therefore, while some dividends are allowed, any surplus above this cap has to be recycled back in to the community. The asset lock concerns the ability of directors to transfer the assets of the CIC, essentially preventing the CIC brand being abused. For example, if there were no asset lock, a CIC could be set up and run ostensibly in the interests of the community and its assets subsequently transferred to a corporation, which is then sold. Any 'social capital' built up through the operation of the CIC would then be capitalised and sold, which defeats the purpose of the CIC.

The relatively short history of the CIC is informative in at least three ways. First, the creation of statute concerned with CICs reinforces an important theme of this book, that the evolution of the economy frequently throws up new challenges to statutory law. Social enterprises emerged from within society, and the organisational forms available prior to 2004 were unsuited. The CIC was an appropriate reaction. Second, the drive to create the CIC came from the Cabinet Office in conjunction with two knowledgeable members of the public and not the Department for Trade and Industry (the DTI, which is now the Department for Business, Innovation and Skills, or BIS). We argue in the concluding chapter that BIS ought to be tasked with facilitating a surveillance exercise to monitor the changing nature of the economy, in order to catalyse new organisational forms when they are appropriate.

Importantly, we are not saying that the idea for new forms like the CIC necessarily ought to come from within government. Far from it in fact: it is essential that the government does not control and own such dialogues – it should however raise such questions continuously and it should also leverage the creative ideas of the population. We consider this issue of economic surveillance and social dialogue further in Chapter 7.

The third point is that organisations are about more than just profit. Financial returns are one of many values that individuals and organisations embody. There are others, including contributing to one's community, which is a value that is embodied in many charities and IPSs. In a sense, the need for the CIC form arose from the need to marry a new type of organisation with the values of people wishing to run social enterprises.

Concluding Comments

This chapter has drawn out some important history concerning the organisations that have emerged in the UK over the past few centuries. We have also highlighted particular points, such as the relationship between statutory law and uncertainty, which we will develop in the next chapter.

4

Organisational Law and the Dynamic Economy

In this chapter we will outline some general points that emerged from the discussions of legal history in the last chapter. Where appropriate, we will interlace these with some concepts from the new paradigm of dynamic networks, which we have now mentioned several times.

The Evolution of the Political Economy & Stakeholder Engagement

It is important not to focus purely on the legal and economic history of organisational forms but to look at the wider political economy when trying to understand the historical emergence and evolution of such forms. For example, we saw in the last chapter that charity law emerged in the 16th and early 17th Century when Elizabeth I sought to control the charitable activities of the church. This historical feature of economic evolution resulting from a political economic process dovetails with a lesson for the policy making process from the new paradigm of dynamic networks. This is the idea that the formation of new policy, including new statutes, *ought* to involve and emerge from, a collaborative process among all relevant stakeholders within a policy domain.

Consultation is widespread in a lot of government policy formation but we would note that the old economics paradigm tends to emphasise two broad points that might run counter to collaborative processes. First, economics is typically treated as a distinct domain kept separate from political ideologies and values, as if politics were polluting in some way. In certain circumstances this is useful;

61

however, it is also worthwhile creating a broad dialogue among stakeholders, which might be viewed as 'political'. Second, the old economics paradigm tends to be orientated around experts having the 'right' model of the economy, with data being plugged in to models that then generate some policy outcomes. In this broad approach, dialogue among stakeholders isn't necessary because the economic model is known. In the new paradigm, an economic system is seen as both highly complex and evolving, and this means there are no objective, 'correct' models of the economy. For policy formation this means that various perspectives ought be drawn together in a collaborative way in order to make sense of the whole terrain. Again, this can be seen as a 'political economic' process.

We should be clear, however, that we are not arguing that all economic policy questions should be fully politicised. For example, there are good reasons why the Bank of England should remain broadly independent of political influence. Our point is more one of emphasis, that the new paradigm argues for broad-based collaboration when forming new policy. This will help to enable the creation of new organisational forms.

The Role of the Law Concerning Organisations

In light of the history of organisational forms and the law pertaining to them, we would define the role of organisational law as *establishing the rights & responsibilities of all of the stakeholders concerning an organisation, in order to mitigate uncertainty for those stakeholders*. We use the term stakeholders in a broad sense, including everyone that is affected by the existence or dissolution of the organisation, however indirectly.

This group typically includes shareholders, creditors, suppliers, clients, directors and other employees, contractors, and the tax authorities. However, we would add the *general public* to this traditional list of stakeholders because organisations do not exist in a vacuum. There are a number of positive and negative externalities that arise from the relationships between an organisation and society at large. For example, when a company fails and is placed into administration, often there are negative externalities that cascade through the economic system. For instance, if a major car plant is closed in a region of the country, this often results in a large number of people being made redundant. Invariably, the taxpayer is negatively affected because of the unemployment and housing benefit payments that follow such large-scale redundancies, which is in addition to any tax revenues that might be lost. This inclusion of the general public among stakeholders is important in our discussion about moral hazard in the next chapter.

Common Law, Statutory Law and Uncertainty

A detailed discussion of common law and statutory law, including the difference between them, is beyond the scope of this book. However, there are a number of important points we will make here. Most importantly, we believe that statutory law has a particularly important role to play in mitigating the *current and future* uncertainty faced by organisations. The nature of dynamic networks is such that uncertainty is inherent in the economic process, so it can never be eliminated; however, statutory law has an important role in reducing uncertainty for organisations and their stakeholders.

As we noted in the last chapter, common law might seem much better suited than statutory law to the evolution of organisational forms in the economic process. Common law is about ground-up, emergent processes and it is based on precedent arising from case law. By its nature, common law evolves over time to suit contemporaneous circumstances because judges have a certain amount of discretion to interpret any precedents that emerged through history. Judges can also accommodate any idiosyncrasies in particular cases. These features of common law lead it to being well suited to evolving economic and social systems. However, we would argue that common law does an imperfect job of mitigating the uncertainty that organisations face in a *dynamic* economy. This is especially true when new industries are emerging and when the economic system is in a state of rapid change as happened during the industrial revolution and, we believe, is happening today.

The main problems with common law are two-fold. First, as we stated in the last chapter, it is in effect backward looking, with *current* precedent having emerged from *historical* case law. Judges do have discretion in current cases but this point nevertheless holds true. The second problem is that new precedents arise out of new case law, which requires cases to be brought before a judge. What this means, in effect, is that common law operates with a lag. This creates problems for the owners and managers of organisations operating in a changing economy because nobody wants to be the first to set a new precedent. This can be thought of as a free-rider problem. All in all, these two problems emphasise that common law can be inadequate at the frontier of change.

Given this tension between an evolving economy and lagged common law, there is a strong argument that statutory law should take on the role of ensuring law concerned with organisations reduces uncertainty as far as practicable. To do this it must remain relevant and, to the extent it is possible, to account for possible future states of the economy. We saw in the last chapter three good examples of statutory law being used to reduce uncertainty and to encourage particular forms of activity. The most prominent example was the creation of the Joint Stock Company Acts of 1844 and 1856 and the Limited Liability Act of 1855. These acts played an essential role in reducing uncertainty for owners and investors, which helped to further catalyse the industrial revolution. The second example was the Industrial and Provident Societies Partnership Act of 1852; and the third example was the Companies (Audit, Investigations and Community Enterprise) Act of 2004, which created the CIC.

A further objective of statutory law concerned with organisations should be, we would argue, for it to be sufficiently comprehensive so that non-legal experts can understand the main principles at least. In chapter 2 we discussed natural cognitive limitations and how people develop expertise. Clearly, most people are not legal experts, and this includes many of the owners and managers of organisations. It would be self-defeating if statutory law were incomprehensible to lay people because that would create uncertainty. Clearly, we are referring here to a general understanding of law: people will inevitably have to refer to lawyers when more complex circumstances require it. Within this discussion, there is an important question about whether it is possible for those constructing statutory laws to know how to write them in such a way as to reduce uncertainty. We believe that it is, as exemplified by the three new organisational forms cited above, the most recent being the CIC.

From the perspective of dynamic networks, a pattern recognition process is required whereby law writers engage in a dialogue with the general public in order to understand the emergent and emerging patterns in the economy. This should not be mistaken for some expert drafting a model to describe the economy without engaging with the public. In effect, the CIC emerged from two knowledgeable members of the public recognising a need for a new organisational form given the changing patterns of the economy, and a counterpart awareness in the Cabinet Office. So it was two members of the public – not a so-called economics expert – who felt that a new form would help to mitigate uncertainty in the present and in the future, in a way that was helpful to various stakeholders. It is important not to conflate this important question about writing laws and uncertainty with the issue of self-regulation. That discussion is often held within a static framing of the economy in which there are few or no information asymmetries. Here we are not talking about regulation and self-regulation in this way.

Overall, therefore, we are arguing that statutory law should be constantly under question to ensure that it is befitting of today's economy and, to the extent it's possible, encouraging and not restricting tomorrow's economy. This warrants society at large constantly questioning the relevance of statutes in the context of the changing economy, a process in which the government should have a role. We would argue, however, that the government should not fully own and control this process, which we discuss further in the concluding chapter.

Conservative and Progressive Law

We mentioned briefly in the last chapter that common law could be viewed – broadly speaking – as a conservative form of law, whereas the role of statutory law was to be relevant and appropriate to the contemporaneous economy i.e. it has a progressive role. We do not mean these words in the political sense. In addition, we do not mean that common law does not progress (it clearly does), nor that statutory law is never grounded in historical legal principles.

To understand the importance of this need for law to be both conservative and progressive, we can delve a little deeper into the nature of dynamic systems. On the one hand, existing institutions, laws, and patterns of behaviour (including norms) have enormous social value, which means we need to be careful – or conservative – when seeking to change such things. On the other hand, the nature of the economy evolves over time, for example because of technological changes, which means institutions, laws, and patterns of behaviour might become obsolete. Therefore, laws need to be periodically renewed to ensure they remain relevant i.e. they need to progress. The point is that the conservativeness and progression need to co-exist in a dynamic economic network. They are a complementary pair.[1]

Indeed, we would offer the following quote from Adam Smith, who wrote along similar lines to the point we are making here.

> The proposal of any new law or regulation of commerce ... ought always to be listened to with great precaution, and ought never be adopted till after having been long and carefully examined, not only with the most scrupulous, but with the most suspicious attention.[2]

Protecting Statutory Brands

Another way in which statutory law does and ought to mitigate uncertainty concerning organisations is to protect the 'brand name' of certain organisational forms. We referred to this problem in the last chapter when we noted how, in the 1930s, unscrupulous people incorporated investment funds as IPSs. This helped them to avoid publishing certain information. This is a problem because certain types of organisations, notably charities and IPSs, have pro-social objectives. This is an important part of their brand identity, and brands play an important role in conveying information to people in a simple way i.e. they have social value. The wider public is familiar with the brands of organisational forms, for example we all know that charities do charitable work. It is important, therefore, that statutory and regulatory law is designed to ensure not only that that there are no abuses but also that these brand identities are protected.

The Meaning of Law to Different People

In dealing with the role of law concerned with organisational forms, it is worth highlighting another similarity between the new paradigm of dynamic networks and the writings of Adam Smith. While Smith is generally acknowledged to have catalysed the classical paradigm of economics, it is ironic that a great deal of his writing sits comfortably with the new paradigm. This includes his views on jurisprudence, which were best represented in *The Science of the Legislator: The Natural Jurisprudence of David Hume and Adam Smith* by Knud Haakonssen.

Smith's overall view was that laws should not be viewed as mechanical constraints on people, which is often the case with economic and legal theories that came after Smith. In large parts (though not all) of the social sciences, societies are treated as if they are static machines and people as if they were cogs in that machine. We would argue that this is broadly consistent with neoclassical economics. Within this mechanistic framework, laws are set and the role of the legislative system is to impose incentives on people to ensure that they comply with these laws. The idea is that people weigh up the costs and benefits of conforming to – or breaking – the law, which means the government has to calibrate incentives to ensure people follow it.

This framework, however, fails to recognise something that Smith did, that people are idiosyncratic and that they can view the law in many different ways. The new paradigm of dynamic networks leads us to a similar view, namely that the law means different things to different people. Some people view laws as equivalent to universal natural law, to be followed under all circumstances; others will weigh up the potential costs and benefits of breaking the law, to arrive at an informed view; and others will view laws as constructive forms of self-organisation in dynamic networks.

It becomes more complicated than this when we accommodate some of the lessons of modern neuroscience and cognitive science which stress that people hold multiple narratives and identities. Work by Bruce Hood (e.g. his popular book, *The Self-Illusion*) suggests that in reality people are a bundle of identities and life-narratives, and that they can switch between identities. As a result, individuals might view the law differently depending on their circumstances. We would argue that in addition to thinking of people as idiosyncratic (and not as homogenous cogs in a machine), it is also preferable to think of the law as a part of the enabling and constraining environment of social systems. When we think of a dynamic network of broadly autonomous individuals interacting with each other, we can see that various things influence behaviour, including ethical and moral factors, norms, and the laws of the land.

This subject area is large and complex, and we cannot do it justice here. But a policy implication of these points is that the government should ensure that new laws concerned with organisations account for such idiosyncrasies; and that laws are appropriately enabling and constraining. In the context of organisations, we argued in Chapter 2 that a fundamental role of organisational law is to enable two important features of organisations, namely the combination of specialisation and integration, and creativity.

The Economics of Organisational Forms, Profit, and Pro-Social Aims

Broadly speaking, the 'economics' of some industries lead them to be suited to particular organisational forms.[3] For example, many accounting firms are partnerships in part because their industry is largely about human-intensive processes orientated around personal relationships between colleagues and clients. In addition, the economics of this industry mean that firms require little outside investment and, therefore, little investor protection compared with industrial-type companies. As a result, few accounting firms are incorporated as joint stock companies.

Equivalently, particular industries are more suited to the joint stock company form, notably those with substantial capital requirements. We have made this point several times already. Therefore, when it comes to profit-seeking behaviour, different forms might be suited to different industries, or several types of industry. We would not, however, assert this point about alignment between industries and organisational forms too heavily. There seems to be a fairly loose association, which merely ought to be acknowledged. Furthermore, if we step back from the profit motive and consider values in a more general sense, we see that some forms, notably IPSs and charities, include pro-social values. The people running these organisations have different objectives e.g. IPSs exist for the good of their communities, and charities exist to do charitable acts. This implies that there is a broader alignment between the values of particular groups of organisations, such as IPSs and charities, and organisational forms.

If we view the economy as an evolutionary process in which new industries arise and die, we can see clearly a major rationale for there being an evolutionary *legislative* process. Moreover, as new industries emerge, new organisational forms might be warranted. These points lie at the heart of our thesis in this book. We will look at this further in Chapter 6 in the context of newly emerging patterns of relationships like we see with co-created common assets (e.g. Linux).

Lock-In

One of the issues that a government would have to consider if it thought of the economy as a dynamic network is the concept of *lock-in*. As the term implies, particular patterns of behaviour can get locked into dynamic networks over time, which can be difficult and costly to get out of. In terms of organisational law, what this means is that particular forms of organisation will persist for at least two reasons. First, case law will build up around statutes, which helps to reduce any uncertainty regarding particular pieces of legislation e.g. the various companies acts in the UK will have been tested many times in the courts, leading to clarity about the meaning of these statutes. Second, this reduction in uncertainty will – other things being equal – lead to newly formed organisations being attracted to these forms over other, less certain, forms.

Together, these two trends will lead to particular organisational forms being locked in to some degree. This is re-enforced by a point raised above, that the neoclassical paradigm assumes a static economy, which reduces the tendency of a government to question the relevance of the forms that exist at any point in time. We would argue that the joint stock company is one such 'locked-in' form. It should be clear, in light of the discussions about LLPs and CICs, that we are over-generalising here because new forms *have* emerged over time. However, we would argue that in reality the CIC is the only genuinely new form of organisation to have emerged over the past 150 years because the LLP largely copies the joint stock company model. It looks to be mostly a hybrid between general partnerships and joint stock companies.

Over a long enough time period, locked-in forms might eventually sit awkwardly with the real world, which will inevitably evolve. If statutory law were equivalently evolutionary, we would see statutes – like that which created the CIC – emerge periodically, and for other statutes to become obsolete. Finally, it would appear that the joint stock company is often treated as if it somehow corresponded to free market economics and/or that it is a natural phenomenon. We would emphasise that it should not be viewed in either way: the joint stock company was created in the late 19th Century to reduce investment uncertainty vis-à-vis industrial organisations. As stated earlier, it is a human construct. For policy making, the main implication of lock-in for a government is that it has to maintain a balance between any social value attributed to lock-in as a result of reduced uncertainty, and any tensions that might arise between existing forms and reality. At the moment, we would argue, public policy does not inherently recognise the need to allow organisational forms to emerge – changes tend to arise only out of crisis.

A Dynamic Economy Versus a Static Paradigm

One of the key tensions in the formation of statutory law in the UK today is that the economy is an inherently creative and evolutionary system; whereas the economics paradigm most prevalent in government policy is based on static systems. One of the policy conclusions we flesh out in the final chapter is that the government and the civil service ought to think of the economy as an evolutionary process. This will require them to reduce their emphasis on an old paradigm orientated around neoclassical economics.

Clearly, this point is broader than just statutory law concerned with organisational forms. The old paradigm is present across many (if not all) of the corridors of Westminster, in a wide variety of domains. We should emphasise once again, however, that we are not arguing the old paradigm has *no* value, we are merely arguing that when policy makers are questioning policy which involves the economy as an evolving system, they ought to use a more relevant framework. This is certainly true of statutory law concerning organisations. Furthermore, this shift in thinking ought to form the basis of a type of economic surveillance concerned with organisational forms. Within this there are three key questions: are the statutes that exist today relevant? Do any existing statutes need updating? And are new statutory forms necessary, as the economy evolves?

Statute Obsolescence

In the next chapter we will look more closely at some of the problems attributed to joint stock companies. Many issues have been raised about such corporations, including the moral hazard problem due to limited liability, which we have alluded to already, and the declining ability of shareholders to control the board of directors. We would set this discussion in the broader context of what happens when statutory law concerned with organisations appears to be obsolete. After all, problems with particular statutory forms might arise simply because they now appear inappropriate in the face of economic change. In these circumstances, a fundamental challenge is to ascertain why this is the case.

There are three broad approaches a government could take. The first is to re-write the statute to try to make it more relevant to today's economic circumstances. The Companies Act has, for example, been revised on many occasions over the years. The second approach is to consider instead whether a new form of organisation is warranted. The third approach is to combine the first two.

In terms of the joint stock company, there is an argument that the various problems that have arisen are because this particular form was appropriate for the industrial economy but as we move further into a post-industrial world, it is starting to look obsolete. Has the economy changed so much that we should in fact stop reforming the Companies Act and instead look to create new organisational forms that are more befitting of a post-industrial economy?

5

The Joint Stock Company

So far in this book we have emphasised the idea that the economic process is fundamentally an evolutionary one and, if the economy is evolutionary in nature, so too should be the statutory process concerned with organisational forms. In addition, we have argued that the role of statutory law should be to mitigate the uncertainty faced by the stakeholders involved in organisations. Metaphorically, organisational forms play a role similar to that of species in natural selection and, over a long enough time period, we should expect new species to emerge and for those species no longer suited to the environment to die away.

In the last chapter we asked the question of what should happen when problems emerge with some organisational form. Should we seek to re-write the relevant statute or should we allow it to become obsolete? In this chapter we will focus on the joint stock company, starting with a number of well-known problems in the first part of the chapter. In the second part, we consider how best to proceed in light of these problems, arguing both for new forms to emerge and for particular reforms to the Companies Act.

Some Problems with Joint Stock Companies

There are a number of issues concerning the joint stock company, about which a great deal of literature exists. In this section we will emphasise:

1. The Principal-Agent problem between owners and managers;

2. The Free-Rider problem, which limits dispersed shareholders from acting collectively in several ways;

3. A Prisoners' Dilemma effect within investment management, whereby competition drives down the resources devoted to shareholder action;

4. A conflict of interest between investment managers who are also non-executive directors;

5. The problem of moral hazard due to limited liability, which is particularly acute in banking;

6. The profit focus, which can give way to environmental and social externalities.

The first three of these six fall under the umbrella of 'corporate governance', being largely about the control over single companies by shareholders. The last three are about the impact that joint stock companies have on the wider world.

1. Owners, Managers and Management Incentives

The Principal-Agent problem arises in the domain of corporate governance because of what Adam Smith referred to as far back as *The Wealth of Nations*:

> The directors of such companies, however, being the managers rather of other people's money than of their own, it cannot well be expected, that they should watch over it with the same anxious vigilance with which the partners in a private copartnery frequently watch over their own.... Negligence and profusion, therefore, must always prevail, more or less in the management of the affairs of such a company.[1]

This problem arises from what economists refer to as 'information asymmetry' between owners and managers whereby it is inevitable that managers will know more about the corporation, including its commercial environment, staff, etc., than the owners. This puts them at an advantage over the owners, which, depending on the scale of the information gap, allows managers to pursue their own aims. This has led to a great deal of literature about aligning the incentives of managers with those of the owners, in addition to different tools for doing this e.g. share options.

2. Dispersed Share Ownership and the Free-Rider Problem

A second traditional problem with joint stock companies is that of dispersed share-ownership, which creates a free-rider problem among shareholders. Consider, for example, if the shares of British Petroleum were spread among thousands of shareholders, the largest of which owned, say, 5% of shares. The incentive of any single shareholder to act on corporate matters is extremely weak relative to a shareholder that owns, say, more than 50% of voting shares. The free-rider problem means that, in effect, each shareholder is incentivised to wait for others to act. Clearly, if all shareholders adopt this stance then the control of shareholders over managers will be very weak. Of course, we are not saying that this caricature is accurate for all shareholders in all companies but it is an important issue for many. In one sense, this free-rider problem can be viewed as a *collective action problem* because it represents a failure of shareholders to act collectively, in a way that would be in their own interests. This leads us to consider the means by which collective action can be enabled among shareholders, which is a question we take up below.

3. Resources Devoted to Shareholder Action by Investment Managers

The third problem with joint stock companies we would highlight is that competition between investment management companies – those who manage other people's shareholdings – for business can drive down the resources devoted to shareholder action. In part this could be viewed as a manifestation of the free-rider problem noted above if shareholding clients preferred their investment managers not to participate in shareholder action, especially if it meant reduced fees.

But, to the extent shareholders and trustees do care, often the resources devoted to this exercise are hidden behind several layers of relationships i.e. there is another information asymmetry problem. For example, many pension funds have several thousand members and a board of trustees to oversee the management of the fund, and a separate investment management team responsible for the day-to-day management of the assets. This leads to several 'walls' of information asymmetry between the ultimate members of the fund and its management; and shareholder action is one area where costs are easily reduced. It is not uncommon, for example, for UK pension funds to have a single investment manager responsible for several hundred shareholdings, leaving a minuscule amount of time available to shareholder actions for individual companies.

We should emphasise, however, it is not true that there are no resources devoted to shareholder matters in investment management companies. Some do take the matter seriously and view it as a part of their job, notably larger investment management firms whose aggregated shareholdings, which might be spread across several funds, are material. However, many firms put few resources into shareholder action, which is sub-optimal at the aggregated level because it weakens shareholder control over managers. Hence it is comparable to the Prisoner's Dilemma in game theory.

4. Conflict of Interest Between Investment Managers and Shareholders

It is not unusual for senior investment managers in investment management firms to take on non-executive directorships. This is true of a broad range of joint stock companies – large and small – and it is particularly prevalent among private equity funds. The managers of these funds clearly wish to have a say in the strategic direction and management of the companies in which they have invested. We would argue that the involvement of investment managers in small companies in which they hold private equity is entirely reasonable; but, to a degree, the inclusion of investment managers on boards in which the funds they manage have no interest can create a conflict of interest, albeit indirect.

For example, investment managers have an indirect interest in ensuring that directors' remuneration is very high. What this means is that they will be incentivised to argue against (or at least not argue for) pay being curbed in the companies whose shares they might manage. We should emphasise and acknowledge that this effect is somewhat indirect but it is a factor that ought to be taken in to account. Directors' remuneration is not set for specific companies in isolation from others: it is normally set according to the 'going market rate' and investment managers with non-executive posts will have an incentive to ensure that the market rate is high.

Executive Pay

So far in this chapter we have outlined four problems with the joint stock company. Even taken in isolation, each of the first three weakens the power that shareholders have over the managers of joint stock companies. Taken together, they lead to a substantial weakening of this power. These factors lead to less shareholder oversight over *specific* companies; but we would also argue that this has enabled certain themes to emerge across firms. Most notably, the remuneration of directors and other senior managers within firms has risen substantially over recent decades and we think this is in part due to the weaker grip that shareholders have over the companies they own. In fact, we would argue that the remuneration of many executives has lost touch with reality, exceeding any reasonable estimate of fairness.

This excessive remuneration, and the detachment of pay from added value, was best demonstrated in the financial crisis when the executive directors of large banks like RBS, which had to be rescued by an injection of public funds, left these organisations with large pay-outs. The most notably example was Fred Goodwin who resigned as CEO of RBS in October 2008, walking away from the bank with a pension equivalent to approximately £8mn. Goodwin oversaw the bank's aggressive corporate strategy for several years prior to the financial crisis, which led to it being vulnerable to such shocks.

5. *Limited Liability, Moral Hazard & Investment*

A fifth problem traditionally discussed in this field, which we have referred to already in this book, is the problem of moral hazard due to limited liability. This is sometimes referred to by the phrase 'private profits, public losses' and it captures the idea that limited liability is like an insurance policy, limiting the liability of shareholders to their initial investment, and limiting the recourse of creditors to the net worth of the company. For readers familiar with finance, shareholders are in effect given (i.e. free of charge) an equity put option with a strike price of zero. With insurance comes moral hazard, and depending on the nature of the business and the risk tolerance of the investors, this can lead to excessive risk taking.

Many people have argued that limited liability lay at the heart of the financial crisis which began in 2007: employees of banks knew that any losses incurred from taking large bets would be constrained by their organisation's limited liability. Moreover, the idea of 'too big to fail' added to this: so the downside was protected both by limited liability and an expectation that the larger banks were too large to fail. With the exception of a few banks like Lehman Brothers, this proved to be largely correct. The financial crisis had many more facets to it and we think it would be preferable to view limited liability as one factor contributing to the risks taken ahead of the crisis. For the purposes of this book, we need only take away the idea that limited liability is like an insurance contract, which can be exploited by the owners (and employees) of companies.

Put another way, the moral hazard effect due to insurance can lead to behaviour that has negative externalities: when a company goes bankrupt, this can cause a ripple effect in the economy whereby others lose out, such as the company's suppliers. It is important to understand, however, that limited liability has value if it helps to mitigate uncertainty and encourage investment in the economy. This was the prime advantage of joint stock companies being allowed to have limited liability in the first place. It should be obvious that investment has been a fundamental feature of the British economy since the beginning of the industrial revolution. In fact, it is one of the main reasons for the high standards of living we enjoy today in Britain. Investment helps to provide the capacity for organisations to 'explore the space of possibilities' and to be creative in order to innovate. It has been, and remains, an *essential* part of the economic process.

Moreover, one of the lessons of the new paradigm of dynamic networks is that uncertainty is inherent in the economy. And investors are on the whole known to be averse to uncertainty. Therefore, limited liability has been an essential ingredient in reducing the level of uncertainty that investors have faced since the second half of the 19th Century. So, while moral hazard is a noteworthy problem, it is important to emphasise that limited liability has a mixed scorecard, which leaves us to question whether it is possible to keep the positive aspects and to mitigate the negative. One idea is to force companies to pay for the insurance implicit in limited liability, which we discuss further below.

6. Single Bottom Line

A common critique of joint stock companies is that prioritising financial returns over all other factors can lead them to make decisions that are environmentally damaging and/or anti-social. The standard policy response from a neoclassical economics perspective is to attach property rights to the environment, allowing a market for externalities to emerge. If property rights are not feasible, the government should impose rules in the form of laws or regulations, which include appropriate incentives to help achieve some outcome. In the neoclassical world, either of these should be sufficient to prevent the negative externalities due to joint stock companies pursuing solely profit maximisation.

But while markets for externalities and government dictat can help to mitigate these problems, we would argue that these tools will never fully *solve* all such problems. Representatives of companies engage in highly localised interactions, in the moment, and many such interactions in the real world are not fully open to influence by legal rules or property rights. Put another way, not all decisions by employees can be anticipated ex ante and known about ex post, rendering it impossible to codify rules in order to influence behaviour. This leads us to question whether ethical principles have a role to play in mitigating these externalities, and whether it would ever be possible to enforce such things. We take this up in the next section, noting that in fact the Companies Act 2006 already includes these features.

Moving Forward With Joint Stock Companies

The section above was a *tour d'horizon* of the main problems with the joint stock company, which are well known. In the next two sections we will consider further the question of what could be done in light of these problems. We recommend a two-pronged approach. First, we will argue for certain reforms to joint stock companies, which correspond to the problems described above. We discuss these in this section. Second, we recognise that the joint stock company model was designed for an industrial era and that shareholders may now wish to consider alternative organisational forms. This second point re-iterates a theme running throughout this book, that there needs to be a wide variety of forms available to would-be owners and directors of organisations from which to choose. These points are taken up further in the final section of this chapter.

Principal-Agent 'Solution'

Of the several problems outlined above, perhaps the one most inherent, and therefore most difficult to overcome, is the information asymmetry that exists between owners and managers. We cannot foresee that this problem will ever be fully 'solved'. The two broad approaches to mitigate this problem involve either companies publishing more information for shareholders and other stakeholders to see; or for the incentives of managers to be aligned with shareholders. Today, companies have to produce a substantial amount of information, much of which is vetted by independent auditors. We would add an optimistic point here too, that the information and communications revolution of recent decades is making the world less opaque, which includes the actions of joint stock companies. This revolution should help to reduce the information asymmetries under discussion.

The traditional way in which managers' incentives are aligned with that of shareholders has been through share options being given to executives and other senior managers. In fact, we would question the dominant corporate policy of aligning managers' remuneration with the *gross* share price of a company because it makes more sense to base incentives on *relative* share price performance. The main reason for this is reinforced by the new paradigm in economics which suggests that asset prices are formed not only from 'economic fundamentals' but also from the complex interplay of many parts of the economic and financial system.[2] Others have also stated a preference for managers' rewards to be based on relative performance (e.g. Milgrom & Roberts in *Economics, Organization and Management*) so this point is not new. Our point here is merely to emphasise that the new paradigm supports the idea of relative performance.[3]

An additional effect of remuneration based on relative share performance might be to reduce the overall remuneration of executives. Stock options involve asymmetric rewards that can be enormous during asset bubbles (which might lead to executives exercising their options) but without equivalent losses during crashes. This asymmetry is a feature of options, which we might think of being like a lobster pot. Therefore, stock options can be viewed as a means for executives to benefit from asset price bubbles. Relative performance metrics can be designed so that they do not have the same asymmetry built in to them, which might lead to lower overall remuneration.

Collective Action

The free-rider problem discussed above raises the question of whether there are any mechanisms that might enable collective action among shareholders. In fact, there are such mechanisms already, known as *shareholder proxy firms.*

These companies either directly represent shareholders in corporate matters i.e. they cast their clients' votes, or they provide advice about voting only. The two largest companies in this field are Glass, Lewis, and Co. LLP[4] and Institutional Shareholder Services (ISS)[5]. However, the existence of these proxy firms does not guarantee that shareholders will act collectively; they merely provide the option. In fact, and most importantly, the existence of such firms does nothing to overcome the free-rider problem we identified above.

We would argue for the use of *financial regulations* to require investment management companies to do one of two things: either to take an active role in shareholder affairs or to lodge their shares with shareholder proxy firms who would vote on their behalf. We expect that this would lead to a much larger number of investment managers lodging shareholdings with proxy firms in order to mitigate the cost and distraction of voting in shareholder matters. In order to catalyse (but not to fully manage) this process, there is arguable a role for the newly formed *Financial Policy Committee*. Indeed, we would also promote collusion among larger shareholders and proxy firms in order to aggregate the power they have over the executives of a company. Collusion typically sits uncomfortably in a broadly free market system but in this case it has value because it would be in order to counter the power of executives.

We would note briefly that a form of collective action has arisen recently in an attempt to reduce executive pay, led by the Secretary of State for Business, Innovation and Skills (BIS), Vince Cable. BIS published a paper in March 2012 on executive pay, which in effect called for curbs on excessive remuneration.[6] We would hold this up as a type of meta-collective action, organised at the national level, and believe that such an exceptional measure has arisen in part because of the lack of effective oversight of shareholders over the past few decades. This attempt at national collective action sits well with our recommendations. In addition, our recommendation for collective action among investors sits well with the *Kay Review of UK Equity Markets and Long Term Decision Making*, which published its final report in July 2012. A general recommendation contained in that report was:

> There should be more opportunity for collective action by asset managers who should have greater freedom to act collectively without fear of regulatory consequences.[7]

More specifically, the Kay Review recommended that an investors' forum should be created,

> ...the objectives of which are to facilitate both supportive and critical action on issues of concern to investors, in general and in relation to particular companies.[8]

While the Kay Review was focused on the specific question of long-term investment, its recommendations for collective action emerged from a similar analysis of the problems with corporate governance, including the free-rider problem. We support these recommendations wholeheartedly.

Investment Managers Holding Directorships

In the first part of this chapter we discussed the indirect conflict of interest that investment managers have if they hold non-executive directorships. With the exception of private equity funds, we propose that investment managers are barred from taking on non-executive directorships. There is a strong rationale for private equity investment managers to take on such directorships, and we would not interfere with that. Therefore, we propose that investment managers are not allowed to be non-executive directors of companies that have a turnover of more than, say, £10mn (a more precise figure would have to emerge from deeper research). We believe this rule would detach investment managers, whose main responsibility should be to their clients, from any conflict of interest arising from being non-executive directors.

Moral Hazard & Insurance Premiums

As we mentioned in the first part of this chapter, limited liability has a mixed scorecard because it has the beneficial characteristic of reducing uncertainty for investors but it can also lead to moral hazard. There are two possible ways forward with limited liability. The first is to revoke the concept and return to the unlimited liability of the early 19th Century and before. We would argue against this because limited liability has helped to help reduce investment uncertainty concerning industrial firms. Moreover, rather than fundamentally redesigning the joint stock company, it would be preferably to develop new forms of organisation without limited liability as a feature, leaving the joint stock company form unchanged.

The second option is to recognise that limited liability is equivalent to a type of insurance for shareholders, and to design a system in which companies are charged for the privilege of limited liability status i.e. to pay an insurance premium. The guiding principle would be that the insurance being paid for would correspond to the negative externalities arising from insolvency. We would recommend such a system because it retains the uncertainty-mitigating feature of limited liability while also mitigating the problems arising from moral hazard. The insurance premiums would be pooled and used when companies are put in to administration upon insolvency, to pay for the associated costs. Indeed, in designing this limited liability insurance we would further recommend that this system is designed and run in a way similar to third-party car insurance. The main role for the government would be to make it a legal requirement that companies with limited liability must have this insurance, as it does with car insurance.

Furthermore, we would argue that creditors charging a market interest rate to the company for their credit, notably the providers of loan capital, should not be covered by this third-party insurance. This is because market interest rates include an implicit insurance premium in the form of the interest rate premium charged over the risk-free rate, to cover the possibility of default (and other risks). If such creditors were covered by the third-party limited liability insurance that we propose, they would be insured twice over. This is an important point that would mean substantially lower insurance premiums than if such creditors were included. We would *not* recommend that the government operated such an insurance system because insurance companies have much greater expertise in this area.

It is reassuring that the market for car insurance is buoyant, highly competitive, and can handle the idiosyncrasies inherent in car insurance. Those readers with cars in the UK will be familiar with the extensive questionnaires required in order to get such insurance. We envisage a similar system emerging in limited liability insurance whereby insurance premiums will take in to account a range of factors related to the business. Curiously, one of the criticisms of this policy from our colleagues is that this policy would lead to moral hazard-type behaviour. Our response is that *moral hazard already exists* so the payment of insurance premiums is merely the counterpart to it. There is, however, a legitimate question of whether such insurance payments would induce firms to act more irresponsibly. This is possible but we suspect the effect would be marginal.

Moreover, it makes sense for financial institutions to be treated differently from other companies in terms of limited liability insurance. There are two broad reasons for this. First, it is questionable whether insurance companies ought to buy limited liability insurance from other insurance companies. There are potential network cascade effects here i.e. a potential domino effect in the insurance industry. Second, we view banks as a unique entity in the economy because of the integrated nature of today's financial system and because many banks are viewed – justifiably – as too big to fail. As mentioned above, this augments the moral hazard effect of limited liability. The banking industry is so special in fact that we would call for a new organisational form that is written specifically for banks.

Dealing with Network Cascades

The negative externalities involved with insolvency are much more complex than we have discussed thus far. In large part, we have mostly implied that the externalities involved in a company going bust would be isolated to its immediate counterparts. The new paradigm of dynamic networks, however, would lead us to consider the potential role of companies in network-wide cascades. Such cascading effects often happen in recessions when the insolvency of, say, a large company leads to the insolvency of its smaller suppliers. Recessions can often involve broad based cascades as multiple insolvencies result in further multiple insolvencies. Therefore, the negative externalities of one company becoming insolvent can extend well beyond its immediate environment.

One of the potential benefits of limited liability insurance would be to help mitigate these cascading effects. Small creditors like small business suppliers to larger companies that go bust would receive greater compensation under this system than without it, which would help prevent them becoming insolvent. Limited liability insurance would in effect take on the role of fire-breakers in forests, helping to enhance the resilience of the whole system.

Externalities and Ethics

It is very common to assume that the directors of companies incorporated under the Companies Act 2006 only have a duty to the shareholders leading them to pursue shareholder returns only. It is noteworthy, however, that the Companies Act 2006 includes the following text with respect to the duty of company directors:

172 Duty to promote the success of the company

(1) A director of a company must act in the way he considers, in good faith, would be most likely to promote the success of the company for the benefit of its members as a whole, and in doing so have regard (amongst other matters) to —

   (a) the likely consequences of any decision in the long term,
   (b) the interests of the company's employees,
   (c) the need to foster the company's business relationships with suppliers, customers and others,
   (d) the impact of the company's operations on the community and the environment,
   (e) the desirability of the company maintaining a reputation for high standards of business conduct, and
   (f) the need to act fairly as between members of the company.[9]

We would highlight subsection (1)(d) above, which states that company directors have a duty to have regard to 'the impact of the company's operations on the community and the environment'.[10] We would argue, however, that this is almost certainly not being rigorously enforced, and that in large part, directors prioritise the financial returns to the shareholders above non-company values. We would propose four things here. The first is to change the wording of the above text to something like the following:

> Company directors have a duty to take reasonable steps to ensure that the company's operations have no undue negative impact on communities and the environment.

The aim here is to balance three different things. First, a number of joint stock companies are very large and directors cannot fully control other employees. They can only influence them. It is unreasonable, therefore, to expect that directors take full responsibility for all of the actions of all employees. Second, and nonetheless, directors should be responsible for taking reasonable steps to make it clear to other employees that the organisation should abide by this principle. Third, the wording should not lead directors to be so risk averse that the company doesn't do anything at all. When looked at close enough, most actions of most organisations will have social and environmental impact – the aim should be to ensure no unreasonable and preventable negative impact.

It is important that we emphasise the notion of 'reasonable steps' here because on the face of it, these policy options might appear bureaucratic. They are not meant to be: they are intended to balance social and environmental protection against the costs of doing business. A second proposal is to introduce independent audits in the domain of such community and environmental damage. There are clearly information asymmetries in this domain, and independent auditors can play a useful role in mitigating these. The third proposal is to ensure that this duty of directors is strongly enforced i.e. that companies are prosecuted when it is clear beyond reasonable doubt that they have damaged either the environment or communities in an undue way. Over time, case law would build up, making it clearer what this section of the Companies Act means. Importantly, this would not involve only the public sector enforcing the law via criminal prosecution; it would also allow civil cases if, for example, a local community felt a company had broken the law.

A fourth proposal is that prosecutions should be directed towards the company rather than individual directors who are acting on its behalf. This is an important point because, if directors were directly prosecuted, it would probably make it difficult for companies to recruit capable people in to these jobs. Clearly, if a company is rightly prosecuted and a specific director is to blame then the company's internal processes would have to handle any subsequent internal punishment, including sacking.

Developing New Forms

We have by now mentioned several times the idea that a range of organisational forms should exist from which owners can choose, and that these forms ought to be under regular review. Put another way, we would promote an active and buoyant market for organisational forms, which would be a sort of *meta-market* existing 'above' the various competitive markets in which individual organisations operate. As we have stated several times, there is an important role for the government here since it is statutory law that would enable such a buoyant market.

There is an important question, however, about private and public costs in this area because some owners and directors will probably be more attracted to organisational forms that enable them to pursue profit only rather than forms which internalised externality costs. These externalities include possible environmental and community damage when companies are a going concern, and potential losses that arise from insolvency under limited liability. In the concluding chapter, we argue this is a 'level playing field' issue and that all organisations should be subject to the various proposals we outlined above concerning moral hazard and social and environmental impact. For the remainder of this section, we will discuss briefly a number of specific new forms which might help owners mitigate some of the problems with joint stock companies mentioned above. In the next chapter we will focus specifically on the new, emerging economy that we emphasised in the opening chapter, and ask whether we need to consider new statutes to enable this new economy.

A Triple Bottom Line Company

In the absence of the Companies Act wording proposed above, concerning the environment and communities, and in the absence of this being effectively enforced, there may be room for an organisation that is explicitly pro-social, pro-environmental, and which is at least financially viable. This is typically referred to as a 'triple-bottom line' approach. Importantly, and as should be obvious by now, we are not arguing that this type of company should replace the joint stock company as it currently exists. We are arguing that such a form should be considered as a new type, to be designed and supported by statute, which would run alongside the joint stock company.

The newly created CIC seems to broadly embody these multiple values; however, the emphasis of the CIC is more about communities, and specifically (though not entirely) local communities. Therefore, we feel that the CIC in its current form does not do what we have in mind. The rationale for this new form does, however, tie into the rationale for the CIC, which we believe was due to an evolution of values within British society. Notably, this involved an increased desire for people to own, work in, and transact with organisations that are not purely profit-orientated. The social enterprise movement is a key part of this. Clearly, and in light of our comments above concerning private aims and public costs, there is a legitimate question of whether enough business owners would make use of this new form to make it worthwhile in the first place e.g. incurring the costs of writing statutes. This is a legitimate question and one taken up in more detail in the final chapter. Fundamentally this is about balancing the costs of such a legislative approach against the costs of the current system, which can perpetuate obsolete forms and frustrate the emergence of new economic activity.

In any case, there is a good argument that competitive pressures might lead some joint stock companies to switch to this new form. If UK values have evolved to increase the desire for organisations that are explicitly triple-bottom line, customers might begin to ask why organisations currently in the form of joint stock companies were not operating under this new form: 'Are you anti-environment and anti-community?'. We should emphasise that this new form might not revolutionise business in the UK immediately, or even substantially. Its success would depend on a number of factors, most of which are unpredictable. But we see that it might well constitute a form that befits our evolving values: society would decide.

A Company with a German-Style Governance Structure

There is an age-old debate that centres on the question of whether UK joint stock companies should take on some of the governance features seen on the continent, notably in Germany. These features mostly involve multiple stakeholders being embedded into the governance of companies in a way that is not typically seen in Anglo-

Saxon countries. A detailed analysis of this is beyond the scope of this book but we would note that Germany's governance structure includes three different bodies and processes:

1. an annual general meeting of shareholders, which has certain rights to make certain decisions, laid down in statute;

2. a management board, which is in effect the *executive* directorship of the company; and

3. a supervisory board, which oversees the management board and appoints its members.

   Three key features of this approach are:

   (i)   the inclusion of employee representatives on the supervisory board (up to one half of the board);
   (ii) separation of the management and supervisory boards; and
   (iv) the prevention of simultaneous membership of the supervisory and management boards.

Many of the discussions about the German governance structure in the UK have asked whether the Companies Act should be re-written to force joint stock companies to take on these features. Again, the idea here is not to replace the joint stock company in its current form but to allow the emergence of a new form that would run alongside it. There is again the question of whether the owners of current joint stock companies would want to adopt any of the principles of the German approach, or whether people would choose this form when setting up a new company. After all, allowing worker representatives on to a supervisory board would probably reduce the overall power that shareholders have to influence the company they own.

A key reason why shareholders might in fact choose this form is to mitigate the power of the executive directors. There is full separation between the supervisory and management boards and the former chooses the latter. There is a second argument, which might lead owners to choose such a structure. It might in fact make a company more competitive for reasons we highlighted in Chapter 3 concerning policy formation. This is the idea that the new paradigm of dynamic networks emphasises, which is the value of engaging multiple stakeholders when tackling some problem. Often there is no single way of looking at some issue or problem, which means there is often value in listening to multiple perspectives, from multiple stakeholders. If so, corporate governance that is structured this way might make a company more competitive. At the very least, the owners of companies should be given the choice between different approaches encapsulated in different organisational forms.

A New Banking Form

The third new form we would propose in this chapter is one dedicated to banks. A detailed discussion of the problems with the banking sector is well beyond the scope of this book. But here we would merely like to recognise that banks are special because they are deeply integrated in to the British economy to such an extent that most banks are too big and too interconnected to fail. As a result, there is an argument that banks should be subject to a statute which is tailored to their unique characteristics.

Moreover, we would further argue that banks should also be subject to the limited liability insurance premium we discussed above. However, in the case of banks, we believe this premium should be paid to the government. This is to recognise that in the event of a systemic banking crisis, it would be the government that would step in to rescue the banking system, with funds provided by the taxpayer. Insurance companies are unlikely to be able to provide the capacity to rescue the banking sector in the case of multiple insolvencies – that role should rest with the government as it did during the recent financial crisis. The insurance premiums paid should correspond to the potential cost of a system-wide rescue. We envisage these premiums being substantially greater than the banking levy currently being paid by banks, which is currently set at 0.13% of the global balance sheets of UK-based banks.

6

The New Economy

So far in this book we have emphasised that the economy is an evolving process, and that statutory law concerned with organisations should evolve in a complementary way. We have also mentioned that, today, the global economy seems to be going through a transformation as significant as the industrial revolution due to computing technology. In this chapter we will drill further down into this last point and ask whether a new organisational form is warranted in light of the new, emerging economy. We argue that it is.

The new paradigm of dynamic networks tells us that if the economy is perpetually evolving, then its patterns of interaction will also constantly change. What this tells us is that in order to understand the economy at any point in time, we have to conduct a pattern-recognition process from the ground up. We do something like that in this chapter.

In fact, in one sense this chapter is a pilot version of the process that needs to happen on a perpetual basis, for which we believe BIS ought to have a leading role. This involves:

(i) Economic 'sense-making', involving the identification of new underlying features of the economy, including new technology;

(ii) An identification of new patterns of relationships in the economy;

(iii) Questioning whether new forms of organisations are warranted in light of (i) and (ii), and questioning existing statute.

The structure of this chapter is broadly in line with these three points. In the first section below we will describe some of the features of the new economy, which differs in significant ways to the industrial economy. The second section describes one of the emerging patterns of interaction within the new economy, involving entities that hold 'common' socially valuable assets; and distributed enterprises, many of which simultaneously co-create and make use of these common assets for commercial purposes. The final section focuses on the required characteristics of the 'commons' entity in particular, which the P2P Foundation refers to as a *for-benefit corporation*.[1]

Before moving further, it is worthwhile noting that the nature of the new, emerging economy is so different to the old, industrial economy that it seems to have jumped considerably far ahead of the economics profession. This should not be surprising during periods of fundamental change in which new patterns emerge that look very different to previous frameworks of reference. But it makes the job of making sense of the 'new' much harder because often we inadvertently look to old theory to understand new patterns of behaviour.

Furthermore, as we stated in the opening chapter, we seem to be undergoing an economic epoch change, which involves not only a shift in the real economy but also a new paradigm in the economics profession. The paradigm of dynamic networks we have referred to many times in this book is much more conducive to making sense of the new economy, although that does not necessarily mean it is easy to understand.

Features of the New Economy

Below we have identified seven features of the new economy. We should emphasise that this list constitutes one particular description: there are many other legitimate ways of expressing the same features. For example, in the first edition of their book *Wikinomics*, Don Tapscott and

Anthony Williams identified four broad trends: being open, peer-to-peer interaction, sharing, and acting globally. We have incorporated these into the seven features described below, although we should also recognise that the first version of their book was published in 2006, which, as far as the new economy is concerned, was the Dark Ages!

Another point to emphasise is that, conventionally, the economics profession seeks to differentiate between 'positive' and 'normative' statements. We might think of positive statements as objective hypotheses that can be tested e.g. lower interest rates will increase house prices, while normative statements involve subjective value judgements which cannot be tested by referring to empirical evidence e.g. blue is a nicer colour than red. However, we do not think such a stark division is appropriate here. Many of the new principles of the new economy are also bound up in culture change, including a newly emerging set of values. Indeed, for many, the new economy represents a counter-culture movement 'against' the now highly centralised industrial economy. We think it would be wrong, therefore, to entirely separate 'positive' principles and any associated 'normative' values. A further point is that here we are focusing on an emerging part of the larger economy: we are not claiming that the whole economy is changing in this way. It is preferable to think of this as more like a new sector of the economy.

(1) Technology Change: Networked Computers

If there is one defining characteristic of the new economy, it is the enabling role of computing power, and the technology that allows computers to be networked together. Networked computers represent the technological change that is the driving force behind the new economy. An excellent account of the role of technological change in a dynamic economy was provided by W. Brian Arthur in his book *The Nature of Technology*. Arthur's views on technology were heavily influenced by his immersion in the study of dynamic networks. In his book he discusses how new technology is built out of the old, in a creative way.

Networked computers are themselves innovations but they can also be viewed as platforms for further innovation. This is most obvious when it comes to software. Computer hardware enables the transfer of digital information; operating systems are designed in order to translate programmes into this digital language; and software is written in different computer languages (such as C++). So the new economy we are referring to includes networked computers and the software which is written and used on those computers. We use the term 'computers' in a very general sense, including devices such as mobile phones, tablets, laptops, desktops, and servers. An excellent example of the new economy is the combination of the operating system used on many *smartphones*, known as *Android*, and the enormous number of *apps* (software applications) that are tied into this operating system. Note that Android's operating system is based on an older operating system known as Linux (which is open-source).

(2) A Change in the Nature of Scarcity & Ownership

Most people define economics as being about *the allocation of scarce resources*, which are commonly viewed as natural and labour resources. Scarcity is therefore deeply embedded in the economics profession. The nature of scarcity in the new economy appears somewhat different to the industrial economy, which was largely material in nature and therefore it was (reasonably) concerned with the scarcity of material resources.[2] There appears to be two aspects to this. First, the marginal cost of replicating many things in the new economy is so trivial that we may as well consider them to be zero e.g. the cost of storing this book on a typical hard drive is about 0.006 pence and the cost of storing an average 2 hour movie is about 6 pence. This is because what we consider to be of value in the new economy involves fewer material resources than in the industrial economy.

Second, scarcity in the industrial economy is not only about natural resources, it is also about the creation and protection of intellectual property (IP). In effect, firms seek to *create* scarcity in order to profit from it. We should emphasise we are not being critical here: this system has been very important in incentivising people and firms to be creative and to develop new technology, which is then patented. We would probably not have the standard of living we have today in the UK without this system. Indeed, it is questionable whether the new economy would exist at all without these incentives, which included protection by IP and patent laws.

By contrast, the new economy involves a great deal of shared IP. In fact, the term *intellectual property* seems inappropriate when it comes to open-source software like Linux since these are awkward bedfellows. It is preferable to think of Linux as a form of *common property*. Furthermore, and importantly, we are not saying that the new economy is all about sharing. If we recall the smartphone-Android-apps combination above, it is clear that IP laws protect many apps. The operating system (Android) is, however, open-source. Furthermore, we would highlight the existence of creative commons licenses[3], which are a noteworthy part of the new economy. At the time of writing there were six types of license, all of which permit the sharing of the licensed material but with different forms of restrictions concerning attribution, variation, and commercial use. These licenses are now being extensively used within the UK economy. This sharing feature of the new economy, enabled by technology like creative commons licenses, makes it substantively different to the old economy.

(3) A Blurring of Production and Consumption

Generally speaking, life in the industrial economy was split between production and consumption. Most people did work that generated income but which they would have preferred not to do; and then they spent that income on various goods and services, which they enjoyed. This dichotomy has been embedded in the microeconomic foundations of neoclassical economics for over a century, whereby agents consider their potential remuneration and their preferences, and then choose an optimal balance between work and leisure. In fact, it was this framework that led some economists at the time of the Great Depression to claim that the persistent unemployment observed at that time was due to people voluntarily going on an extended holiday.

This distinction between production and consumption has become blurred in the new economy. People have been observed doing things that could be viewed as both production and consumption. For example, if somebody writes an entry in Wikipedia on a subject in which they are an expert, in return for no income, it is production in the sense that others can read and make use of the entry. But it could be viewed as consumption because people often find satisfaction in doing this. Note that we are not claiming this to be true of everybody, nor even a majority of people; we are merely stating what has been observed. Furthermore, we are not claiming such things are confined to the new economy, as it looks similar to old-fashioned acts of charity, albeit in a new guise.

Another common example of production and consumption (which some refer to as *prosumption*[4]) is blogging. Many people blog in their free time, and other people have the ability to read these blog articles via the World Wide Web. Again, we do not want to overstate this – some blogging clearly has a commercial rationale, for example. With this blurring of the lines between production and consumption, we can see again that the old paradigm of economics looks to be far behind. Some research has been done in this area, of course, but the microeconomics of production and consumption continue to form the basis of undergraduate and postgraduate courses in economics.

(4) A Rebalance from Production to Creativity

It is probably not unreasonable to say that the balance of resources employed in the industrial economy *relative to the emerging new economy* is more towards production than innovation, or creativity. Creativity is important in thinking of new products, such as cars, but, post-innovation, a proportionally larger amount of resources are typically devoted to the production process than is the case with the new economy. The industrial economy is balanced more toward production than creativity. To a certain extent, this is also true for skill-based services. Many service-based professions involve the training of experts through vocational training or apprenticeships; and these people then employ the skills learnt in some profession. Importantly, however, there is often a certain amount of creativity at the local level, or 'on the spot', in both goods production and services provision. For example, production lines often throw up small engineering problems that need to be resolved.

In the new economy, the nature of production is considerably different to the industrial economy. Notably, it appears that the balance between people being creative and production is more in favour of the former than the latter. This should not be overstated e.g. many of the apps available via smartphones will have gone through types of production and quality assurance mechanisms. But, on the whole, the new economy allows relatively more time for, and is more about, creativity than the industrial economy.

(5) Peer-to-Peer, Non-Hierarchical Systems

Over-generalising slightly, once a new product has been developed in the industrial economy, industrial methods are then employed to produce it e.g. cars on a production line. The emphasis shifts from being one of creativity to one of production efficiency. Many industrial companies, most of which are joint stock companies, organise themselves along hierarchical lines to ensure this process is highly efficient. A CEO sits at the head of the management team, typically with well-defined lines of reporting and authority running throughout the company. People often compare this management hierarchy structure to a military command structure. There is a deep literature concerned with this approach to management within the management sciences and, in fact, this framework has some broad similarities to neoclassical economics.

The new economy appears to be more about peer-to-peer processes in which forms of self-organisation can emerge from within a community. For example, the creation of Linux was achieved via a highly distributed approach to software writing. But the process was not one of anarchy: within the broad community, the need for collective action and decisions were often identified and handled. As noted above, the new economy seems to be broadly associated with a counter-culture movement, which seems to reject the need for hierarchical systems in favour of devolved, peer-to-peer systems. Comparisons have also been made with the Occupy movement, which also appears to operate with a highly devolved 'model' with no obvious leaders or managers.

This tendency toward peer-to-peer interaction can be viewed as broadly consistent with a greater emphasis on creativity over production. In industrial companies, once a product has been agreed and designed, the challenge is then to execute its production. Hierarchical systems can be very effective in doing this. Of course, one mustn't over-state this: such systems can and do allow some 'toing and froing' between design and production, and in recent decades management science has moved away from this command and control technique. In any case, by contrast, if the new economy is more about creativity and less about production, then hierarchical structures look less appropriate.

(6) Mass Collaboration and the New Commons

Wikipedia is a mass-collaboration exercise *par excellence*. Given its scale, it is remarkable that the Wikimedia Foundation, which 'manages' Wikipedia, had only 65 employees as at May 2011. This compares with approximately 22 million articles online and about 100,000 regular contributors, according to Wikipedia. But, whereas Wikipedia is based substantially on voluntary actions by contributors, a lot of open source software like Linux should be viewed as involving a mixture of voluntary action and self-interest. Here, we do not mean self-interest in a critical way, merely that, in the new economy, motivations are more nuanced. Moreover, a common critique of Wikipedia is to question its accuracy and bias e.g. in the US a number of Republicans have claimed it is biased towards the Democratic Party.

Curiously, the economics of mass collaboration and platforms like Wikipedia bear some resemblance to the economics of 'the Commons' i.e. common land and other resources. An important difference is, however, that in the new economy, resources that have common value are *co-created* through collaborative action. This makes the nature of the 'new economy commons' fundamentally different to the historical question of the commons, which is about the use of an existing finite resource by a group of people with equal access. We argue below that this is an essential feature of the new economy and propose that a new organisational form is considered to meet its requirements.

Perhaps the best example of commons-creating technology is the wiki platform accessed via MediaWikia, which is open source software that forms the infrastructure behind Wikipedia.[5] A 'wiki' is a web-based platform that enables collaboration. In effect, it is a blank version of Wikipedia on which a community can write and co-create content. Wikis can be kept private e.g. in the form of an intranet, or published online.

(7) Multiple Incentives: Voluntary Action and Self-Interest

We have alluded to this final feature of the new economy already in relation to other features but it is worth emphasising in its own right. The new economy appears to exist because of a combination of voluntary action and self-interest. We saw a form of voluntary action at work in the form of 'prosumption' above, and also in the substantial amount of time spent writing Wikipedia entries.

But the new economy is not only about voluntary action. In the model described below we can see that what is emerging in many parts of the new economy is the co-creation of commons-like resources in conjunction with distributed enterprises, which themselves make use of the shared and co-created common resources. Again, the combination of smartphones and Android is a platform that facilitates the creation of apps, many of which have to be purchased (or used free of charge but subject to advertising). It is open to debate whether voluntary action should be included in economic activity but we would argue that it should be, particularly if other people consume whatever is produced.

One Model of the New Economy[6]

The seven features described above represent some very broad brushstrokes of the new economy. In this section we will be more concrete about a particular pattern of relationships that seems to have crystallised in this new economy. The model we will describe in this section is depicted in Figure 2.

Figure 2. A New Economic Model

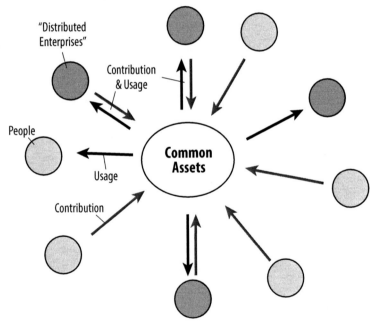

This model includes
(1) Individuals;
(2) Distributed enterprises;
(3) A pool of common assets which sits in the middle of the community.

In order to demonstrate what we mean by this model, we will use the smartphone-Android-apps combination noted above. Individuals and distributed enterprises can have three types of relationships with the common asset pool. They can *contribute* to it e.g. by helping to write and further develop Linux, on which Android is based, or Android itself; they can *use* the common assets e.g. by using Android as an operating system for the creation of new apps; and they can simultaneously *contribute to and use* the assets. The asset pool in the middle of the community embodies co-created common capital, which has broad social value. In our example, Linux and Android are common assets. We should emphasise that the model described here is merely one pattern of relationships emerging from within the new economy. There are others: here we focus on this particular one.

What's Different?

We would argue that, fundamentally, the new economy represents a much more integrated and dynamic network of relationships, and that this is challenging existing organisational form structures. In the industrial economy, under the joint stock company model, a lot of creativity is 'done' internally (or by contractors working for the company). Firms then typically patent this creativity, and then either sell it through products or services, or license it to others. This model balances the surplus profit generated from what amounts to a monopoly with the incentives to innovate that this profit creates. The model depicted in Figure 2 differs from this industrial approach in two critical ways. First, creativity is not internalised: a potentially enormous amount of people can have a say in the common assets pooled in the centre. If this is done well, the creation of the commons assets can benefit from *crowd-sourcing* effects, which can enhance the creativity embodied in the common assets. While taken from a very different context, the phrase 'letting a thousand flowers bloom' is appropriate here.

In addition to this crowd-sourcing effect, the active involvement of users will enhance the development of common assets. For example, distributed enterprises that write apps which run on Android will know better than others some of the features they need built into it. What this highlights is that the value of a common asset is related to the way it is used. In other words, the more deeply integrated are the users in developing some common asset, the more value it is likely to have. So we can see that the new economy model depicted by Figure 2 has the potential to be more creative than the industrial model.

The second way in which this model differs from the industrial model relates to the protection of IP. The first point to make here is that the protection of IP in a digital economy is inherently tricky because, ultimately, digital 'things' (like photographs and software programmes) are easy to copy. Perfect replication is relatively easy, as is replication with some variation in order to mask replication. The second point is a counter-cultural one. Many of the people involved in the new economy, in the development of Linux for example, are vociferously anti-hierarchy and anti-control. Specifically, many see themselves as subverting large joint stock companies like Microsoft and Apple. Moreover, licenses for things like Linux and any of its offshoots ensure that companies cannot own the IP – it must be distributed free of charge. This feature seems to fly in the face of conventional economics.

Importantly, we are not arguing that this model will *necessarily* subvert the joint stock companies working in this domain. The most obvious example of a successful conventional company, which is also a good contrast with the smartphone-Android-apps example we have highlighted, is Apple. Its iPhone is a type of smartphone that uses Apple's own operating system, iOS. Today, iPhones and Android-based smartphones have about the same market share. One argument for why the iPhone might be (at least) keeping pace with Android-based smartphones is Apple's greater ability to integrate its iPhone with its various other devices (e.g. desktop computers and laptops) and other operating systems (e.g. Lion) whereas the smartphone-Android-apps nexus focuses only on one domain. This brings us back to the specialisation-integration feature of organisations from Chapter 2. Given this point about integration, an interesting question is: would a new organisational form help to enable this type of integration among highly dispersed stakeholders? We will not take this question up here – we raise it as an example of the type of question that needs to be asked if a new organisational form is to enable an emerging economy.

Commercial Features

The patterns of relationships described by Figure 2 incorporate a variety of funding models, ranging from a framework based entirely on voluntary contributions to one in which the common assets are fully funded by commercial ventures like distributed enterprises. Other versions might include an amalgam of both. Wikipedia is very close to the voluntary version of this model whereas our running example of smartphone-Android-apps has commercial features that make it more complex. It looks to be a voluntary-commercial hybrid. Clearly, an important challenge for the model illustrated in Figure 2 is to enable a type of collective action which is *financially viable*. The word *viable* is used here because it can include different commercial models.

A New Organisational Form for the New Economy

The P2P Foundation, which is a representative body and champion of the new economy, has argued for the creation of what they refer to as a *for-benefit organisations*, which would 'hold and protect' the common assets described in the model above. This emergence of a new type of organisation out of an evolving economic system is at the heart of this book. We have argued that the economic process is fundamentally evolutionary, and that statutory law, the role of which is to mitigate the uncertainty to stakeholders involved with organisations, ought to evolve in a corresponding way. Here, this leads us to ask: is there a role for statutory law to help enable the type of model described above and, with it, the new economy?

The For-Benefit Organisation

The P2P Foundation has argued for a new form that has the following characteristics:[7]

- Social Purpose. The for-benefit corporation has a core commitment to social purpose embedded in its organisational structure.

- Business Method. The for-benefit corporation can conduct any lawful business activity that is consistent with its social purpose and stakeholder responsibilities.

- Inclusive Ownership. The for-benefit corporation equitably distributes ownership rights among its stakeholders in accordance with their contributions.

- Stakeholder Governance. The for-benefit corporation shares information and control among stakeholder constituencies as they develop.

- Fair Compensation. The for-benefit corporation fairly compensates employees and other stakeholders in proportion to their contributions.

112

- Reasonable Returns. The for-benefit corporation rewards investors subject to reasonable limitations that protect the ability of the organisation to achieve its mission.

- Social and Environmental Responsibility. The for-benefit corporation is committed to continuously improving its social and environmental performance throughout its stakeholder network.

- Transparency. The for-benefit corporation is committed to full and accurate assessment and reporting of its social, environmental, and financial performance and impact.

- Protected Assets. The for-benefit corporation can merge with and acquire any organisation as long as the resulting entity is also a social purpose entity. In the event of dissolution, the assets remain dedicated to social purposes and may not be used for the private gain of any individual beyond reasonable limits on compensation.

It should be clear that the organisation described by the P2P Foundation has a broader remit than the model we described above involving a 'common asset' pool in software-based systems but it is very much consistent with it. We are comfortable with that: the model depicted in Figure 2 can represent a variety of different but similar circumstances in which the creation and protection of a common asset pool might be warranted. For example, employees in the NHS might wish to spin off and operate health care services at the local level, with assets that might be best treated and protected as 'common'. The point is that the for-benefit corporation would be equipped to *enable* the model described in Figure 2, in addition to equivalent patterns of interaction.

Purpose & Brand

The core purpose of the new organisation would be to enable the co-creation of common assets; and it would also serve to hold and protect those assets. In the UK, a number of existing forms share some features with this new proposed form. For example, a fully charitable version of the model could apply for charity status; the community-benefit and the co-operative versions of the IPS appear to broadly fit; and the idea of being for the benefit of the community is consistent with the CIC form. However, none of these forms fit well enough, which justifies a new statute. There is a further argument in support of this when we look at the nature of brand identity and aims. As we stated in chapters 3 and 4, different forms are broadly aligned with different brands. Charities, IPSs, and CICs have clear identities that fit with the values and aims of particular people. This new form, we argue, would be designed to fit with the values and aims captured by the seven features of the new economy described above.

So, the for-benefit corporation would be specifically designed in order to enable the co-creation and protection of common assets, which we believe is sufficiently unique to warrant a new statute. An example of the value of creating a new statute is to reduce the uncertainty about the usage of common assets. Individuals deciding whether or not to contribute their time in order to co-construct such common assets will probably be assured by the support of the law that protected those assets in particular ways. Such protection would include various means to prevent the assets from being capitalised and sold, thereby preventing some individuals disproportionally benefitting from the work of others.

Importantly, there is an argument that common assets such as Linux already exist without this form, so why should we bother? We would argue that Linux exists *despite* there being no for-benefit corporation, and that, given the emerging new economy, more co-created assets would exist if there had been such an organisational form. Moreover, the P2P Foundation is very close to people involved in the new economy trying to work in economic models like that depicted in Figure 2. Their informed judgment is that such a new organisational form is warranted. So, in our opinion, we believe this form would help to further catalyse the newly emerging economy we have described in this chapter.

Policy Proposal

We should emphasise that the precise policy we are advocating here is that BIS should instigate a consultation process to ascertain if a new statute should be written to create the for-benefit corporation. In our best estimation, a new statute should be written that helps to create a new form. But, consistent with the approach of dynamic networks, a thorough consultation process would be necessary, which should involve the engagement of a range of stakeholders. The P2P Foundation is particularly well placed to discuss the intricacies of the arguments made in this chapter.

Would This Add Extra Bureaucracy?

It is self-evident that new statutes should be written with great care and, more specifically, new statutes should not unnecessarily add any bureaucracy to people's lives. Would the for-benefit organisation statute do that? It is important to understand that the drafting of a new statute would merely represent an additional option for people in terms of organisational forms. People seeking to create a new organisation would view this as one possible form among many. It would not be a piece of bureaucracy forced on people across the board.

7

Policy Recommendations

In this concluding chapter we will briefly reiterate some of the policy ideas set out in earlier chapters. In addition, at the end of this chapter we will discuss the idea of overhauling the statutory law in this domain by creating a two-tier system that includes a single Incorporation Act. The main thesis of this book was presented in the opening chapter and emphasised that the economic process is fundamentally an evolutionary one. This stands in contrast to the static nature of mainstream economics, which informs a great deal of government policy. By far the most important recommendation we would make, therefore, is that the government and, more specifically in the context of this book, the Department for Business, Innovation and Skills (BIS), adopts an evolutionary framework in mind when designing policy. All of the analysis and all of the other policy recommendations we make in this book flow from this evolutionary approach.

In Chapter 3 we stated that statutory law concerned with organisational forms is for:

> ...Establishing the rights & responsibilities of all of the stakeholders concerning an organisation, in order to mitigate uncertainty for those stakeholders.

This means that as the economy evolves, it is essential that statutory laws evolve too, to reduce preventable uncertainty. Existing statutory law, therefore, must be questioned on a regular basis to ascertain whether or not it does this. It is also important to question whether the evolving economy warrants *new* forms emerging in the same way the CIC emerged about 10 years ago. We discuss this in more detail below. In Chapter 6 we supported a particular new form, the for-benefit organisation, for precisely this reason.

In Chapter 2 we proposed that a useful way of thinking about organisations was to view them as being about the integration of specialists and specialised technology, and as platforms that enabled creativity. These are not the only features of organisations but we view them as essential, and government policy in general terms should either enable these features and/or reduce as far as possible any constraints that act on them. The vision we would promote, given these points, is that of a healthy, vibrant ecosystem of organisational forms. Or, put another way, we wish to bring about a robust market place for different types of organisations.

Within this vision, it is important to appreciate that some forms might not be 'successful' if success is measured by total population or output. Some new statutes might prove wildly successful, others might prove irrelevant. In dynamic networks, it is impossible to know for sure, before the fact, what will be successful. Another way of thinking about this is to say that new forms should 'explore the space of possibilities'. The point is that BIS needs to be open to exploring different forms, and to recognise that some will 'fail'.

Economic Surveillance & Organisational Forms

If the economy is constantly evolving and new patterns of relationships emerging, then it is essential that as a society we identify these changes and react in appropriate ways. In the context of this book, this means questioning old organisational forms and considering new ones. We prefer to state this point as a challenge for the UK economy because, as we stated in an earlier chapter, it is essential that the government does not fully own and control this process. We believe it would be preferable to think of BIS as leading and hosting a conversation among all relevant stakeholders, and to leverage the value of crowd sourcing such conversations.

In Chapter 3 we described some of the history behind the CIC, noting that the then Labour government had identified a 'gap in the market' for an organisational form that might benefit the emerging social enterprise sector. But it was two members of the general public, Stephen Lloyd and Roger Warren-Evans, who provided the concrete idea. We would propose that BIS is explicitly tasked with leading this type of surveillance on a continuous basis. It would involve not only consideration of the economy as an evolving process (or as a dynamic network). It would also require very deep pattern recognition skills, which in this instance would involve an appreciation of how the law, the economy, technology, and many other aspects, all relate to each other.

Proposals Related to the Joint Stock Company

In Chapter 5 we focused on some of the notable problems with the joint stock company. In response we proposed the following:

- It makes more sense for stock option incentives to be based on the performance of a company's share price *relative* to its peers or some appropriate benchmark.

- Laws and regulations should actively encourage collusion between shareholders in order to balance the power of executives.

- Investment management firms should be required by regulations to either directly participate in shareholder actions or to lodge their shares with shareholder proxy firms who would vote on their behalf.

- Investment managers should be barred from holding non-executive directorships with the exception of private equity fund managers.

- The government should make it a legal requirement that corporations with limited liability must hold 'third party' insurance to mitigate the negative externalities associated with limited liability. Financial regulations should ensure the market for such insurance is enabled.

- The wording of the Companies Act 2006 relating to directors' duties to communities and the environment should be changed to:

  'Company directors have a duty to take reasonable steps to ensure that the company's operations have no undue negative impact on communities and the environment.'

- This new wording should be enforced with greater rigour than the current wording is at present.

- Independent auditors should be used to test compliance with this wording.

New Forms

In Chapter 5 we also proposed three new forms, which would sit alongside (not replace) joint stock companies:

- A triple-bottom line company that would capture emerging values in the UK whereby some people prefer to do business with, own, and work within companies that go beyond the profit motive.

- A company with a governance structure that involved shareholder representatives and other stakeholders, including the workforce. This is broadly comparable to the German governance structure.

- A specific form for banks.

- In Chapter 6 there was a more detailed analysis of the rationale for a new type of organisation that would reflect the newly emerging economy, namely the for-benefit organisation. This has been promoted by the P2P

Foundation and would enable new patterns of relationships in the co-creation and protection of common assets.

A Single Incorporation Act?

In Chapter 5 we mentioned that some owners of organisations would prefer organisational forms that maximize profit at the possible expense of communities or the environment. Put another way, they might prefer to avoid the costs of internalising externalities. In that chapter we referred to this as being about a level playing field for all organisations. This means in fact that the wording used above regarding the duties of directors of companies ought to apply to *all* organisations and not only those incorporated under the Companies Act. This wording is already implicitly or explicitly built in to some statutes concerned with other forms, including charities, CICs and IPSs; however, we believe it is reasonable to propose that all organisational forms are subject to this wording, or equivalent. Unfortunately, if this is to be done, many acts of parliament would have to be re-written.

Moreover, Appendix 1 describes the various organisational forms that exist in the UK today, which includes various types of incorporation and a wider array of forms recognised by statutory law but which are not types of incorporation. This latter group includes charities and CICs. What is described in Appendix 1 is a highly complex picture, which, we would argue, adds to the general uncertainty about the broad landscape of organisational forms. In light of these two points, we would ask whether this landscape should be rebuilt in such a way that makes it much less complex; in a way that would allow for level playing field issues to be addressed effectively; and so that any future changes required for all organisations could be done efficiently. In Chapter 6 we discussed newly emerging patterns: it is possible that some new patterns might emerge where the best response would be for all statutes concerned with organisations to change simultaneously.

One way of doing all of this would be to redesign the legislation so that there was only *one* form of incorporation (requiring an 'Incorporation Act') which would be complemented by a second 'tier' of statutes that would represent the various forms in existence. Every incorporated organisation would be required to abide by the Incorporation Act and an additional single piece of legislation which would be tailored to their organisational type. In effect, this second tier would be a 'bolt-on' to the Incorporation Act. This new framework would reduce the complexity and uncertainty concerning organisational forms, and it would help legislation to evolve, such that changes can be made to influence all organisations and specific organisational forms with the minimum of fuss. In the first instance, the transition to this new framework can be designed to arrive at broadly the same set of organisational forms we see today. For example, the combination of the Incorporation Act and a statute designed for private and public companies could in effect replace the Companies Act 2006. What happens then would depend on how the economy evolved.

Benefits and Costs

In previous chapters we referred to the various costs and benefits of the approach we have advocated in this book. The question we must ask is whether the various proposals of this book are worthwhile given the various costs and benefits. We believe they are. Perhaps the most significant benefit of the approach we suggest is to position the UK's economy so that its organisational forms are relevant to the current and emerging economy. There are significant costs to having obsolete statutes, notably in frustrating newly emerging economic activity. The for-benefit corporation, for example, could help catalyse the co-creation of valuable common assets. Conversely, there is a cost in not having such a form.

There are two further types of costs we should consider this regard. The first is the costs of the type of economic surveillance and consultation exercise we propose, plus the costs of administration in BIS, including writing new statutes and keeping older ones up to date. We are not convinced that this process will be any more or less costly than what is currently spent on organisational forms. The second type of costs is incurred by organisations themselves. It includes legal costs and also costs relating to any uncertainties arising from the law. We suspect that the streamlining of the legislation concerned with organisational forms would ultimately reduce these costs. Moreover, the aim of our approach is specifically to mitigate uncertainty for organisations. Our best estimate, therefore, is that once a fixed cost is incurred in moving to the new system, notably the re-writing of statutes and the drafting of a new Incorporation Act, this new system will probably cost as much as the current system. But it will have clear benefits in enabling new economic activity.

Appendix 1
Organisations – Forms and Participation in the Economy

This Appendix has two parts – the first sets out a typology of organisational forms and the second part looks at the participation of the various forms in the economy. The second part was difficult to write because there was no single database from which to generate comparable data. However, that section includes some of the 'least-bad' data available from various sources.

Part 1 – Typology

There are many ways to categorise organisations and in this section we present what works best for this book. A difficulty is that various existing forms do not sit neatly in to one particular 'type' e.g. an organisation can be a social enterprise, an industrial and provident society (IPS) and a co-operative all at the same time.

Dimensions

It is best to consider three broad dimensions that characterise organisations.

1. *The Nature of Incorporation.* In this book we are mostly interested in incorporated organisations i.e. those with a distinct legal identity. But some organisations have no legal status: their status as an organisation is merely through perception by people in general. An incorporated organisation has a legal status equivalent to that of an individual human being. Furthermore, we refer to a third category of 'floating forms', which includes those forms which do not constitute a formal type of incorporation but which can take on various incorporated or unincorporated forms. Charities are a

good example of a floating form because, currently, they can be incorporated in several ways (e.g. a company or an IPS), and they can be unincorporated too.

2. *Aims*. The broadest aims possible in one organisation can be characterised as a 'triple bottom line' (or 'Profit, People, and Planet') where the organisation aims to achieve financial viability and pursue social and environmental values too.

   At the two ends of a spectrum are private corporations, which will typically pursue profit only, and charities, which are non-profit and typically pursue social and/or environmental value. Other organisations will lie somewhere along this spectrum e.g. social enterprises are mostly 'dual bottom line' i.e. financial viability plus social value.

3. *Ownership*. Organisations vary considerably in terms of who owns them e.g. the shareholders in the case of joint stock companies (JSCs); the members in the case of IPSs; and employees in the case of employee-owned co-operatives.

Figure 3. is a visual representation of different organisational forms categorised in to three different types – incorporated, floating, and unincorporated.

For the remainder of this section we have split these organisations into the three types depicted here: incorporated organisations, floating forms, and unincorporated organisations.

Figure 3. Organisational Forms by Type of Incorporation

	Types of Incorporation	Floating Forms	Unincorporated Forms
	Ltd by guarantee		
Companies (Companies Act 2006)	Ltd by shares (private)	Community Interest Co.	Sole Trader
	Ltd by shares (public)	Charity	Normal Partnership
Partnership (LLP Act 2000)	Limited Liability		
		"Co-operative"	Ltd Partnership
Industrial & Provident Societies (IPS Act 1965)	Community Benefit Society		
	Co-Operative Society	Credit Union	
Charity (Charities Act 2011)	Charitable Incorporated Org		Unincorporated Trust
Financial Mutuals (Building Soc. Act 1986)	Building Society		Unincorporated Association
(Friendly Soc. Act 1992)	Friendly Society		
Incorporation by Statute	Statutory Incorporation		Community Groups & Voluntary Orgs
Incorporation by Royal Charter	Royal Charter Incorpoation		

Types of Incorporation

Companies

There are three limited liability company legal structures:

- A company limited by guarantee is owned by its members who are known as guarantors, but their liability is limited to the value of the guarantee, which can be as little as £1.

- A company limited by shares is owned by its members (shareholders) whose liability is limited to the value of the shares, which cannot be traded on the open market.

- A Public Limited Company (PLC) is 'limited by shares' and controlled by its shareholders but it can trade its shares on the open market.

Companies, whether limited by guarantee or by shares, have to abide by the requirements of the Companies Act 2006.

Limited Liability Partnerships (LLPs)

In the United Kingdom LLPs are governed by the Limited Liability Partnerships Act 2000 in Great Britain and the Limited Liability Partnerships Act (Northern Ireland) 2002 in Northern Ireland. A UK limited liability partnership is a corporate body – that is to say, it has a continuing legal existence independent of its members, as compared to a normal partnership which may (in England and Wales, does not) have a legal existence dependent upon its membership.

UK LLP's members have a collective ('joint') responsibility, to the extent that they may agree in an 'LLP agreement', but no individual ('several') responsibility for each other's actions. As with a limited company or a corporation, members in an LLP cannot, in the absence of fraud or wrongful trading, lose more than they invest.

Industrial and Provident Societies (IPS)

An IPS is an organisation undertaking a business or trade that is registered under the Industrial and Provident Societies Act 1965. IPS members benefit from limited liability but do not have all the requirements associated with limited liability under the Companies Act 2006. It has rules of association similar to an unincorporated association. There are two types of IPS:

A *co-operative society* is a democratic organisation based on the principle of one member, one vote – irrespective of how many shares they hold. They are run for the mutual benefit of their members and surplus profits are re-invested in the organisation.

A *community benefit society* needs to show that its activities will benefit the community and not just its members. Such societies are managed by their members and have to submit annual accounts, but can raise funds by issuing shares to the public. Special rules apply regarding how surplus funds must be applied and how any assets remaining after the society is dissolved should be distributed. This type of society must be able to show why it should not simply be registered as a company under the Companies Act 2006.

Charitable Incorporated Organisation

The Charities Act 2006 introduced a new form of incorporation intended specifically for charities that do not want or need the complication of becoming a company limited by guarantee. Currently, charities wishing to be incorporated will have to fulfil two separate requirements. The CIO is intended to provide the advantages of incorporation (such as limited liability) with regulation by the Charity Commission, the Office of the Scottish Charity Register (OSCR) and the Charity Commission for Northern Ireland (CCNI). The change means that a CIO will need to meet less onerous accounting, reporting, filing and governance requirements.

Financial Mutuals

A mutual, mutual organisation or mutual society is an organisation (which is often, but not always, a company or business) based on the principle of mutuality. Unlike a true cooperative, members usually do not contribute to the capital of the company by direct investment, but derive their right to profits and votes through their customer relationship.

There are two types of incorporated financial mutuals:

• Building Societies: By registering with the Financial Services Authority (FSA) and meeting the obligations of Building Societies under the Building Societies Act of 1986, a building society is also recognised as incorporated.

• Friendly Societies: Similarly, friendly societies must register themselves with the FSA and meet the obligations under the Friendly Societies Act 1992. Once successfully registered, a friendly society is also recognised as incorporated.

A third type of financial mutual is generally recognised, which is a Credit Union. In this book we categorise this as a floating form because it is not, technically speaking, a form of incorporation. Credit Unions must be incorporated as an IPS.

Incorporation by Statute

As the title implies, some organisations are recognised as having a legal identity under a specific statute. Examples of this in the UK are county councils, the Channel Four Television Corporation, and the Olympic Delivery Authority.

Incorporation by Royal Charter

This is very similar to incorporation by statute but it results from a formal document which grants a right or power to an individual or a corporation. Often these organisations will have an important institutional position in the country. Examples include the Bank of England, universities, professional institutions, and the BBC.

Floating Forms

Community Interest Companies (CIC)

The CIC is a legal format designed for use by social enterprises. The CIC status can take the form of a private company limited by shares, a private company limited by guarantee, or a PLC. To qualify as a CIC, an organisation's constitution must feature an 'asset lock', which severely constrains the ability of the CIC to transfer assets; and a dividend cap, meaning that profits must in large part be employed in the community's interest rather than distributed to company members. Its aims must also satisfy a 'Community Interest Test' from the CIC Regulator, which assesses whether the activities undertaken by the CIC will benefit the community. Additionally, it must deliver an annual report to Companies House along with its accounts. In order to encourage investment, CICs limited by shares are entitled to pay a dividend to investors but this is subject to the dividend cap constraint.

Charities

The current position is that charities wanting a corporate structure have to incorporate by one of several forms (as a company limited by guarantee, IPS, Royal Charter, or by statute); and they also have to register as a charity (satisfying the requirements of the Charity Commission, the OSCR or the CCNI). However, charities are also allowed to be unincorporated, taking the form either of an unincorporated association or an unincorporated trust. Above we included in the list of incorporated organisations the charitable incorporated organisation, which came into effect in December 2012.

Co-operatives

The term 'co-operative' is a little vague because a 'co-operative society' is one of the two forms that an IPS can take. However, the term can have a much wider meaning, such that 'co-operatives' can also be incorporated as, for example, a company limited by guarantee. In this book, therefore, we refer to co-operatives as a form of IPS incorporation and also as a floating form. Regardless of incorporation, co-operative businesses are democratic member-owned trading businesses. They are usually formed by groups of people with shared goals or particular ethical reasons for wanting to set up a business together. Usually, they are for-profit businesses, though any profits are under the control of the members rather than distributed to external shareholders. Occasionally social enterprises, community projects and not-for-profit organisations are established as co-operatives. According to Co-operatives UK, (an organisation representing cooperatives in the UK) in 2008 there were more than 4,800 cooperatives in the UK employing some 205,000 people and turning over as much as £29 billion annually.

Co-operatives are driven by ethical values such as self-help, democracy and equality. They claim to put people, rather than capital, at the heart of their activities. They are defined by their relationship with their members; so for example, in a 'worker co-operative' the primary members are the employees. Co-operatives are set up, owned and run by their members, and include, for example, credit unions. A credit union gives its members facilities for saving, borrowing and other financial services. Members save together to create a pool of money from which low cost loans are made.

The International Co-operative Alliance (ICA – www.ica.coop) defines a co-operative as an 'autonomous association of persons united voluntarily to meet their common economic, social and cultural needs and aspirations through a jointly owned and democratically controlled enterprise'. There are several types of co-operative:

- A worker co-operative is a business owned and controlled by its employees – some involve every employee in decision making but some, especially as they grow, elect a board or management committee – perhaps the best known is the John Lewis Partnership.

- A consumer co-operative is owned and controlled by its customers – perhaps the best known on the high street is The Co-operative.

- A community co-operative is owned and controlled by the members of a local community and it normally provides services of benefit to that community – credit unions are good examples.

- Secondary co-operatives are businesses set up by other co-ops – such as Suma, a whole food distributor and wholesaler (www.suma.coop), which was originally set up by a number of whole food co-ops.

- A co-operative consortium is where the members are self-employed people or small businesses in their own right, and the co-operative exists to enable these businesses to pool their resources or provide common services, such as group purchasing, in order to reduce costs.

- Multi-stakeholder co-operatives are made up of members from different areas such as employees, customers and the local community.

Cooperatives are different from other organisations. There are seven principles which have been formalised by the ICA that every cooperative should put into practice. A cooperative should have –

- Voluntary and open membership

- Democratic member control

- Fair and equal economic participation for all members,

often with no or limited return on any capital subscribed

- Independence, so that agreements with third parties are done in such a way as to preserve their autonomy
- Provision of education, training and information for members
- Strong links with other co-operatives
- Concern for the community

Credit Unions

As mentioned above, credit unions are typically classified as a type of financial mutual. They are bound by the Credit Unions Act 1979.

A credit union is generally operated for the purpose of promoting savings, and providing credit and other financial services to its members.

Unincorporated organisations

Sole Traders

Sole traders are also known as sole proprietorships or sole operators. This legal status is a common form of business start-up. The legal and accounting requirements are more straightforward and less time consuming than those of a business registered as a limited company. Operating as a sole trader is often a simpler option than creating a limited company because there are no registration fees, and preparing accounts and keeping records is more straightforward. However, unlike a limited company, a sole trader is personally liable for the debts of the business, which means that their home and assets may be at risk. Sole traders often experience greater difficulty raising finance than limited companies. However, being a sole trader means people have complete control over the management of the business and retain all of the profits. There is no distinction drawn between personal and business income so accounting is relatively straight-forward. Sole traders can register for VAT and take on employees. They can also become a limited company at a later stage if they choose to.

Normal Partnerships

Partnerships are a relatively simple way for two or more people to set up in business as there are fewer administrative burdens than when setting up and managing a limited company. A normal partnership is a good legal status to consider if a business will involve two or more people owning it together. The partners are regarded as self-employed. Management of a normal partnership is typically shared between the partners, but this can be varied by agreement. Like sole traders, business partners have unlimited liability for the debts of the business and are regarded as being liable both 'jointly and severally'. This means that all the partners can be responsible for transactions or contracts entered into by any one or more of the other partners.

Limited Partnerships

A limited partnership (not to be confused with a LLP) has at least one normal and one limited partner. A normal partner has management rights and is liable for all the partnership's debts. The limited partner, who may be an individual or a business, contributes a fixed amount (as capital or property) to the partnership, but is only liable for partnership debts or liabilities up to the amount they have contributed.

Unincorporated Trusts

Trusts are unincorporated bodies managed by trustees who are personally liable for the liabilities of the trust:

- Trustees cannot benefit from the trust but must act on behalf of the community
- Trusts establish their own rules for governance
- Trusts have no separate legal identity
- The social objectives of a trust are protected in a trust deed
- Trusts can own assets and property
- Trusts can include an asset lock in their rules to prevent their assets being distributed outside the community that the trust serves

Trusts can be set up with money or shares. Those with charitable objectives can be registered as charitable trusts. The charitable objective must be set out in the trust deed, which describes the framework in which trustees operate.

Unincorporated Associations

An unincorporated association does not have a separate legal identity from its owners. The association normally has a constitution that sets out its aims and objectives, and is run by a committee whose members are all personally liable for debts incurred by the business. Because it has no legal identity of its own, and in legal terms is only a collection of individuals, an unincorporated association cannot start legal action, borrow money or enter into contracts in its own name. It also cannot hold property without appointing trustees (usually committee members) doing so on its behalf.

Community groups and voluntary organisations

Community groups range from small groups run by local people who aim to improve services in their local area e.g. running childcare schemes such as playgroups, or managing village hall facilities for community use. Voluntary organisations are independent and self-governing and act for the benefit of the community for no financial gain. They may employ paid staff or be managed by volunteers.

Part 2 – Participation in the UK Economy
Overview & Focus on Enterprises in General

The following quote is from the ONS publication *Painting Pictures of Place: Business Topic Profile*:

'For the purposes of this article a business is a legally recognised organisation that trades in goods and/or services for financial reward... An "enterprise" is, essentially, a business with a degree of autonomy – usually a head office – which may, or may not, have multiple sites, or "local units". A local unit is defined as the individual business site, located in a geographically identifiable place. Local units are particularly appropriate for location-based analysis of business statistics.

'Four categories of business are featured – sole proprietors, partnerships, companies & public corporations, and general government & non-profit making bodies.

- Of the UK's 2.15 million enterprises in 2009, companies and public corporations represented the largest category by legal status (58 per cent). In the same year general government and non-profit making bodies made up the smallest legal category of enterprises (4 per cent).

- 76 per cent of all enterprises in the UK employed fewer than five people in 2009. Only five per cent of enterprises employed 20 or more people in 2009. There was little geographic variation from the aggregate UK figure, the most notable exception being the North East which had fewer enterprises employing 0 to 4 people than the UK overall.

- The largest broad industry sector in the UK in 2009 was "Professional, Scientific and Technical" at 15 per cent of all enterprises, followed by "Construction" at 13 per cent. There was a wide range of different broad industries in England and Wales in 2009, and this mix was similar for all the English Government Office Regions (GORs).

- The percentages of new enterprises "born", and those that closed or "died" at local authority level in 2008, varied widely throughout England and Wales – although most local authorities saw enterprise "birth" rates of 8 to 14 per cent and "death" rates of 8 to 12 per cent.

- In most GORs, turnover per enterprise was between £1.2 million and £1.5 million in 2009.'[1]

'Sub-national output is described in this report through Gross Value Added (GVA). This is a way of measuring the contribution to the UK economy of individual producers, industries and sectors. It is used in the estimation of national Gross Domestic Product (GDP) and is expressed in monetary terms as well as with indices. The GVA per head of population in the UK in 2008 was £20,520.'[2]

Table 1 – Company Size and legal form (FAME, 2007)

Company legal form	Company Size (000s of observations)				
	0 values	Small	Medium	Large	Total
Private Limited	496	1606	54	26	2181
Guarantee	4	59	2	1	65
Public, Not Quoted	1	5	2	2	10
LLP	1	8	1	0	10
Unlimited	1	3	0	1	5
Public, Quoted	0	0	0	1	1
Other	0	0	0	0	1
Total	502	1681	60	31	2274

Source: BERR, 'UK COMPANY STATISTICS RECONCILIATION PROJECT – Final Report', January 2009, p.8.

Table 1 shows statistics for company size and legal form, dating back to 2007, were compiled by the Department for Business Enterprise and Regulatory Reform (BERR).

Note: FAME refers to the Forecasting Analysis and Modelling Environment, a time-series database.

'The term "dormant" applies to a company that, in legal terms, has "no significant accounting transactions" during a financial year. It is not the same as a "non-trading company", a term that has no legal meaning. No significant accounting transactions means there are no entries in the company's accounting records. The majority of zero values are for dormant companies, and the majority of dormant companies have little or no size information. Hence, dormant companies can be associated with zero or missing values with a reasonable degree of confidence.

'Table 1 shows the legal status of companies recorded on the FAME database, 96% of the total companies in the UK are private limited companies. These are split between small, medium and large companies roughly in proportion to their share of the overall population of companies. Other company types tend to be small, with the exception of publicly quoted companies; these are almost always large.

'Although small companies dominate the population, this does not necessarily translate into economic activity. Table 2 shows the relative impact that the size of companies has on employment.'[3]

'It is clear that, although small or micro companies dominate in terms of number of companies as they make up 67% of the population, they only account for 4% of employment. Employment reporting is disproportionately high amongst large companies. This suggests that, if all companies reported employment then the share of micro and small companies defined by employment would rise substantially.

Table 2 – Company Size by Employment – reported values (FAME, May 2007 and IDBR, September 2007)

Employment	Size	Companies	Companies	Percentage of Companies		Percentage of Employment	
		FAME (000s)	IDBR (000s)	FAME	IDBR	All companies	IDBR
0		N/A	22	N/A	0.95	N/A	N/A
1–10	Micro	56	2074	43.43	89.63	0.73	18.48
11–50	Small	31	176	23.88	7.61	2.8	13.07
51–250	Medium	31	33	23.36	1.43	11.74	11.82
250+	Large	12	9	9.32	0.38	84.75	56.63
Total (000s)		131	2314			29264	28252

Source: BERR, 'UK COMPANY STATISTICS RECONCILIATION PROJECT – Final Report', January 2009, p.8.

'IDBR [Inter-Departmental Business Register, managed by the Office of National Statistics] has a much greater population than FAME and clearly differs with regards to the distribution of companies among the given size bands. The larger dataset shows that those observations that FAME has missed can be mostly attributed to small companies. The IDBR also suggests that FAME overestimates the number of large companies (with regards to percentage of employees). Despite the lower percentage of employees, micro and small companies clearly represent a large number of companies and employees in absolute terms and hence have considerable economic and political significance.'[4]

More recent ONS statistics show that:

'there were 2.08 million enterprises registered for VAT and/or PAYE in March 2011, compared with 2.10 million in March 2010, a fall of nearly 20,000 (0.9 per cent). Between March 2010 and March 2011 there was a reduction in the number of sole proprietors and partnerships, while corporate businesses increased by 0.6 per cent:

- Corporate businesses (companies and public corporations) represented 59.8 per cent of total enterprises, up 0.9 percentage points from the 58.9 per cent seen in 2010.

- Sole proprietors represented 23.3 per cent of total enterprises, down 0.5 percentage points from 23.8 per cent in 2010.

- Partnerships represented 12.7 per cent of total enterprises, also down 0.5 percentage points from 13.2 per cent in 2010.

- General government and non-profit making bodies represented 4.2 per cent of total enterprises, compared with 4.1 per cent in 2010. (p1)

'The professional, scientific and technical sector accounted for the largest number of businesses with 15.9 per cent of all enterprises registered. This was followed by construction with 12.6 per cent of all enterprises registered, and retail with 9.0 per cent. The distribution of enterprises by employees shows that 88.8 per cent had less than 10 employees, and 98.0 per cent had less than 50 employees. Large enterprises, those with 250 or more employees, accounted for only 0.4 per cent of all enterprises. Analysis by age of business shows that 14.7 per cent of businesses were under two years old, and 27.7 per cent were under four years old. A further 44.5 per cent of businesses were 10 or more years old.'[5]

Private Sector Estimates (BIS Release, 2010)

'There were an estimated 4.5 million private sector businesses in the UK at the start of 2010, an increase of 48,000 (1.1 per cent) since the start of 2009. (p1) These businesses employed an estimated 22.5 million people, and had an estimated combined annual turnover of £3,200 billion.

'[At the start of 2010] Almost two thirds (64.2 per cent) of private sector enterprises were sole proprietorships,

27.6 per cent were companies and 8.2 per cent were partnerships.'[6]

'There were an estimated 2.9 million sole proprietorships in the UK at the start of 2010, of which 292,000 (10.1 per cent) had employees. There were an estimated 370,000 partnerships, of which 166,000 (44.9 per cent) had employees.

There were 1.2 million companies, of which 736,000 (59.6 per cent) had employees.'[7]

SMEs and Social Enterprises

From BIS Small Business Survey 2010

Note that the vast majority of Social Enterprises are SMEs, so BIS' report focusing on SMEs is a useful comparator and complement to the ONS data above. They state the following:

'Fifty-nine per cent of SME employers are private limited companies, limited by shares. Larger SME employers are more likely than average to be private limited companies.

'Private limited companies are more likely than average to occur in the production (73 per cent), construction (76 per cent) and business services (69 per cent) sectors. London has a high proportion of private limited companies among its SME employers at 65 per cent, whilst Scotland (45 per cent), Wales (51 per cent) and Northern Ireland (40 per cent) have the lowest proportions. This is in spite of the fact that the size of business profiles between the UK regions are very similar.

'Nineteen per cent of SME employers are sole proprietorships, and 10 per cent are partnerships (excluding limited liability partnerships). The TRAD sector is made up of a higher proportion of sole proprietorships (27 per cent) and partnerships (14 per cent) than is the case elsewhere. Conversely, there are fewer sole proprietorships and partnerships in the production sector (13 per cent and

Table 3 – Trends in Legal Status

Base = all SME employers	All SME Employers	Micro (1–9)	Small (10–49)	Medium (50–249)
SBS 2010. Un-weighted (n) =	3817	1528	1530	759
	%	%	%	%
Private limited company, limited by shares (LTD)	59	**56**	**73**	**72**
Sole Proprietorship	19	**22**	**5**	**1**
Partnership	10	11	8	5
Private company limited by guarantee	3	2	5	6
Charity/Not-for-profit organisation	1	1	2	3
Public Ltd Company (PLC)	2	2	3	4
Limited liability partnership	2	1	2	5
A trust	*	*	*	1
Community Interest Company (CIC, limited by guarantee or shares)	*	*	*	1
Other (e.g. unincorporated associations/ Friendly Society/Private Unlimited Company	1	*	*	*
Figures in bold are statistically significant at the 95% confidence level against the overall finding * = a figure of less than 0.5% but higher than zero				

Source: BIS, 'Small Business Survey 2010', April 2011, p. 9

eight per cent respectively), and in the business service sector (13 per cent and seven per cent respectively).

'Private limited companies have risen significantly from 51 per cent in ASBS 07/08 to 59 per cent in SBS 2010. Conversely, sole proprietorships (29 per cent to 19 per cent) and partnerships (16 per cent to 10 per cent) have fallen significantly over the same time period.'[8]

Social Enterprises

Note that the government estimates that there are at least 55,000 social enterprises in the UK with a combined turnover of £27 billion per year. They account for about 5 per cent of all businesses with employees and contribute £8.4 billion per year to the UK economy – almost 1 per cent of annual GDP (Source: NHS Alliance, 2008). The BIS survey states:

'Twenty-six per cent of all SME employers thought of their business as a social enterprise: a business that has mainly social or environmental aims. This is significantly less than the 29 per cent claiming this in ASBS 07/08, but the same figure as in 06/07.

Table 4 – Social Enterprise Trends

Base = all SME employers	SBS 2010	ASBS 2007/08	ASBS 2006/07
Un-weighted (n) =	3817	7783	8949
	%	%	%
Perceive themselves as a social enterprise	**26**	29	26
Conform to BIS definition of a social enterprise	7	6	4
Figures in bold are statistically significant changes between the 07/08 ASBS and the 2010 SBS			

Source: BIS, 'Small Business Survey 2010', April 2011, p. 15

'These self-defined social enterprises were more likely than average to be found in the North East of England (37 per cent), Scotland (34 per cent) and Wales (32 per cent).

'Thirty-four per cent of businesses founded in the last three years defined themselves as social enterprises, compared to 25 per cent of those founded 10 years ago or before.

'This question was not asked to those businesses that pay more than 50% of profits to shareholders. 19 per cent (weighted) were not asked this question but are still included in the base population.

'Nearly a third of those agreeing with this statement were found in the "other services" sector. Indeed, 55 per cent of all in "other services" thought of their business as one with mainly social or environmental aims.

'The Department for Business Innovation and Skills has a further defined definition of a social enterprise. This requires the enterprise to consider itself a social enterprise as above, but not pay more than 50 per cent of profit or surplus to owners or shareholders, generate more than 25 per cent of income from trading, and therefore having less than 75 per cent of turnover from grants or donation. In addition, they have to think themselves a very good fit with the statement "a business with primarily social or environmental objectives, whose surpluses are principally reinvested for that purpose in the business or community, rather than mainly being paid to shareholders and owners."

'Under this definition seven per cent of SME employers could be considered to be social enterprises. This is one percentage point higher than in ASBS 07/08, and three percentage point more than that seen in ASBS 06/07.7.

'Under this definition 22 per cent of "other services" are classified as social enterprises, six per cent of transport, retail and distribution, four per cent of construction, four per cent of business services, three per cent of production, and two per cent of primary SME employers. There were no significant differences according to the size or age of the enterprise.'[9]

Appendix 2

Senscot.com Article: 'Intellectual ferment poured into CICs!'

Article reprinted with permission.[1]

Intellectual ferment poured into CICs!

*Lawyer **Stephen Lloyd**, one of the fathers of the Community Interest Company, explains how the concept came into being and outlines his hopes for how it will develop*

Social Enterprise magazine August 2006.

Attending the recent conference to mark the first year of CICs was a proud moment. That is because the CIC idea was initially hatched by myself and Roger Warren-Evans, a serial social entrepreneur, in Balls Brothers Wine Bar in Cheapside over a bottle of claret.

The conversation that evening had ranged over a variety of topics. Was the use of artificial legal personality breeding amoral behaviour (a theme well explored in The Corporation by Professor Joel Bukan)?

We had also talked about the decline of the building societies, mutual aid societies and other alternative forms of business organisation which had led up to the mono-culture of modern capitalism of the limited liability company. We were both well able to recognise that the limited company has tremendous strengths. Company law is maintained in good order by regular reviews.

On the other hand Industrial & Provident Societies have been allowed to languish with very little change of their legal structures over many years. In the past 30 years there have been at least six major pieces of company law and none for Industrial & Provident Societies.

Roger and I were also aware of the very active US not-for-profit sector. A raft of public-type activities (e.g. running bridges, harbours, etc) are run by US not-for-profit corporations which are not charities. We were also mindful of the fact that it was more complicated and expensive to set up a social enterprise than it was to form a simple limited company. Why should social entrepreneurs have to pay more in order to acquire a legal format than a normal businessman? They needed a simple and cheap legal form.

The other key issue was that many social entrepreneurs do not want to form charities. Charitable status has huge advantages in terms of the tax and rate relief. However, the status brings with it voluntary trustees who often find it difficult to generate the commitment and involvement necessary to operate a business in the commercial world. Charity-type concerns of governance, process and accountability can often dominate when the crucial issues that need to be addressed are customer satisfaction, cash flow and delivery. A number of would-be social entrepreneurs I had seen had looked very enthusiastic about forming a charity, particularly when they realised the scale of the tax reliefs involved – only to become very downcast when I explained that they had to give their baby away; in other words, that the trustees whom they would have to appoint would form the majority of the board and could sack the creator.

Out of these discussions we hatched a plot. We called it the 'Public Interest Company'. It was to have a number of key features:

1. It was to be dedicated in perpetuity to delivering a public purpose.

2. It would have an asset lock, meaning that its assets were dedicated to that public purpose and if the business was sold the monies that were realised thereby would not

be distributed to shareholders by way of profit or gain but would have to be applied to the public purpose.

3. There would be a cap on the remuneration of director/ employee.

We conceived taking these ideas and grafting them onto the company structure, be it a company limited by guarantee or by shares. That was because company law is kept in good order so most of the problems of companies have long ago been ironed out – banks recognise them and they are cheap and easy to form. The Registrar of Companies is an extremely efficient regulator.

Roger wrote a very good, simple and succinct pamphlet summarising all this and we began a campaign. We ran a few meetings and then, luckily, the government began its review through the Strategy Unit in Number 10 Downing Street of the charity and voluntary sector. We submitted a paper on this backed by the Charity Law Association. To our delight the government listened, more than that they adopted the, idea – except that because Alan Millburn had at that point wanted to call the organisations running foundation hospitals 'Public Interest Corporations' the PIC initials had been taken. So the CIC was born.

One of the most important features of the CIC is that it represents, in the case of a company limited by shares, the first clear statutory check upon the notion of shareholder value. This can be overstated but, nonetheless, in a company limited by shares the directors owe their primary duty to the shareholders to maximise value. The Community Interest Company requires directors instead to serve two masters: the community and the investors. The investors, however, accept a hair shirt; a limited rate of financial return and no capital growth. This acceptance by the investors of limits to their expectations frees the directors to pursue the community purpose.

It has been wonderful to witness the number of CICs that have been established over the past year and the variety of uses that are being found for them: Running Reading, Town Centre, The Artists Collection Society, a range of childcare services – to name but a few.

CICs are fast becoming the best possible vehicle for joint ventures between charities and commercial partners. That is because the architecture of the CIC, with a statutory asset lock and a cap on shareholders' returns, means that charities can enter into a joint venture through a CIC with a commercial partner confident that the legal framework of the CIC will mean that the chance of a charity being an unequal partner in the joint venture is much reduced. On top of that there is the CIC Regulator in the background, able to ensure fair play. The government wants to see more and more services currently delivered by the state taken over by social enterprises, whether in the field of health, education or otherwise. CICs are a very good vehicle for this. They could be financed by long-term bonds giving investors a proper rate of return but where capital growth (if any, particularly from underlying assets) will be used for the social purpose.

We conceived of the CIC as being a simple-to-use legal form for social entrepreneurs. The fact that 400 have been formed in a year demonstrates, I hope, that our hopes-are being vindicated. I look forward to seeing more and more CICs being formed to deliver a variety of activities and reflecting a real partnership between the notions of capitalism and the wise use of money and social return.

Appendix 3

For-Benefit Corporations

The defining characteristic of all Fourth Sector Organisations is that they integrate social and environmental aims with business approaches ... a range of efforts are underway to define the criteria for the archetypal Fourth Sector organisation, which is referred to as the 'for-benefit' organisation or corporation.

Characteristics

Attributes of a for-benefit corporation

The following characteristics of an archetypal for-benefit corporation are offered as a starting vision intended to catalyse further dialogue. With this caveat, a fully realized for-benefit could have the following core attributes:

- SOCIAL PURPOSE. The for-benefit corporation has a core commitment to social purpose embedded in its organisational structure.

- BUSINESS METHOD. The for-benefit corporation can conduct any lawful business activity that is consistent with its social purpose and stakeholder responsibilities.

- INCLUSIVE OWNERSHIP. The for-benefit corporation equitably distributes ownership rights among its stakeholders in accordance with their contributions.

- STAKEHOLDER GOVERNANCE. The for-benefit corporation shares information and control among stakeholder constituencies as they develop.

- FAIR COMPENSATION. The for-benefit corporation fairly compensates employees and other stakeholders in proportion to their contributions.

- REASONABLE RETURNS. The for-benefit corporation rewards investors subject to reasonable limitations that protect the ability of the organisation to achieve its mission.

- SOCIAL AND ENVIRONMENTAL RESPONSIBILITY. The for-benefit corporation committed to continuously improving its social and environmental performance throughout its stakeholder network.

- TRANSPARENCY. The for-benefit corporation is committed to full and accurate assessment and reporting of its social, environmental, and financial performance and impact.

- PROTECTED ASSETS. The for-benefit corporation can merge with and acquire any organisation as long as the resulting entity is also a social purpose entity. In the event of dissolution, the assets remain dedicated to social purposes and may not be used for the private gain of any individual beyond reasonable limits on compensation. (http://www.fourthsector.net/learn/for-benefit-corporations)

Discussion

Formalisation in the Law

'For-benefits are a new class of organisation. Like non-profits, for-benefits can organize in pursuit of a wide range of social missions. Like for-profits, for-benefits can generate a broad range of beneficial products and services that improve quality of life for consumers, create jobs, and contribute to the economy.

For-benefits represent a new paradigm in organisational design. At all levels, they aim to link two concepts which are held as a false dichotomy in other models: private interest and public benefit. for-benefits seek to maximize benefit to all stakeholders, and because of their architecture, they can embody some of the best attributes of other organisational forms. They strive to be transparent, accountable, effective, efficient, democratic, inclusive, open, and cooperative.

For the for-benefit organisation to move from an idealized model to widespread cultural reality, support in the law will ultimately be required. Substantive changes are likely needed in corporate, non-profit, intellectual property, tax, securities, consumer protection and other laws at federal, state, and local levels. A range of promising efforts have emerged in recent years to create such regulatory changes.' (http://www.fourthsector.net/learn/for-benefit-corporations).

Notes

1. The Thesis

[1]   These are enterprises registered for VAT, implying a low but non-trivial turnover. The current threshold at which registration is compulsory is £77,000 annual turnover. The estimated number of sole proprietorships below this level of turnover is well over 2 million.

[2]   A . Maddison, *Monitoring the World Economy*, OECD, Paris, 1995.

[3]   Our colleague W. Brian Arthur has been the leading proponent of increasing returns in economic theory and a leading scholar in the field of complexity theory, having been a founding member of the Santa Fe Institute.

[4]   L. Hannah (1999) 'Marshall's "Trees" and the Global "Forest": Were "Giant Redwoods" Different?' in N.R. Lamoreaux, D.M.G. Raff and P.Temin, eds., *Learning by doing in markets, firms and countries*, National Bureau of Economic Research.

[5]   The technical analysis is available at W Cook and P Ormerod (2003), 'Power law distribution of the frequency of demises of US firms', *Physica A*, 324, 207-212; C Di Guilmi, M Gallegati, P Ormerod (2004), 'Scaling invariant distributions of firms' exit in OECD countries', *Physica A*, 334, pp. 267-273.

2. Organisations

[1]   Instead of 'integration', we could also refer to *collaboration* or *co-operation* within organisations, or the *co-ordination* of separate, specialized functions. For the purposes of this book, these words mean the same thing.

[2]   Here we define resilience as *the ability to recover from adversity*.

[3]   Smith, Adam (1957) Selections from *The Wealth of Nations* (ed. George J. Stigler). New York: Appleton Century Crofts (originally published in 1776).

[4]   Hatch, M., *Organization Theory*, p.162, Oxford: OUP, 1997.

[5]   See, for example, *Organizations in Action*, New York: McGraw-Hill, 1967.

[6]   See, for example, Prof. Allen's paper 'A Complex Systems Approach to Learning, Adaptive Networks' (available at http://once-cs.csregistry.org/ tiki-download_wiki_attachment.php?attId=411).

3. The Emergence of Different Organisational Forms

[1]   Commons Journals xi 696, as quoted in Partnership Law Ch. 01, available at: http://www.bloomsburyprofessional.com/pdfs/PartnershipLawCh01.pdf

[2]   Ibid.

[3]   F. Heaton, 'Financing the Industrial Revolution' in F. Crouzet (ed.), *Capital Formation in the Industrial Revolution*, London, 1972, pp. 88-9.

4 Available online here:
   http://www.legislation.gov.uk/ukpga/2006/46/ contents.
5 The details can be found in this article: http://www.senscot.net/
   view_art.php?viewid=5024, which is also reprinted (with permission)
   in Appendix 2.

4. *Organisational Law and the Dynamic Economy*

1 Sometimes people refer to these as 'dialectical'.
2 Adam Smith, *An Inquiry Into the Nature and Causes of the Wealth of
   Nation* (1776).
3 We are grateful to John Kay for emphasizing this point with us.

5. *The Joint Stock Company*

1 Adam Smith, *An Inquiry Into the Nature and Causes of the Wealth of
   Nations* (1776).
2 In more technical language, we would say that share prices are an
   emergent outcome of network-wide interaction.
3 This point is also captured by the Capital Asset Pricing Model (CAPM),
   which breaks down the performance of a share price in to idiosyncratic
   (i.e. company specific) factors, referred to as Alpha, and systematic
   factors (such as the stage of the economic cycle), known as Beta.
   Curiously, despite CAPM having existed for almost 50 years, this
   distinction has hardly made it in to the design of incentives for
   employees.
4 Glass, Lewis, and Co. LLP website available at:
   http://www.glasslewis.com/
5 ISS website available at: http://www.issgovernance.com/
6 'Shareholder voting rights consultation', March 2012, [online],
   available at: http://www.bis.gov.uk/assets/biscore/business-
   law/docs/e/12-639-executive-pay-shareholder-voting-rights-
   consultation.pdf
7 'The Kay Review of UK Equity Markets and Long-term Decision
   Making', July 2012, p.50 available at:
   http://www.bis.gov.uk/assets/biscore/business-law/docs/k/12-917-
   kay-review-of-equity-markets-final-report.pdf
8 IBID
9 Companies Act 2006, Part 10, Chapter 2, section 172, available at:
   http://www.legislation.gov.uk/ukpga/2006/46/pdfs/ukpga_200600
   46_en.pdf
10 We are grateful to Stephen Lloyd for drawing our attention to this part
    of the Companies Act 2006.

6. *The New Economy*

1 P2P foundation website available at: http://p2pfoundation.net/
2 It is interesting to note that in his book referred to above, W. Brian

Arthur implicitly calls for a new definition of economics. He views an economy as 'the set of arrangements and activities by which a society satisfies its needs', which stands in contrast to a study of the allocation of scarce resources.

3   See: http://creativecommons.org/licenses/
4   This term is used to mean different things. Here we refer to it as the combination of production and consumption.
5   See: http://www.mediawiki.org/wiki/MediaWiki
6   We are grateful to Michel Bauwens, Co-Founder of the P2P Foundation, for his significant contribution to the next two sections.
7   This list is derived from the P2P foundation website: http://p2pfoundation.net/For-benefit_corporations. The whole webpage is reprinted (with permission) in Annex 3.

Appendix 1

1   ONS, *Painting Pictures of Place: Business Topic Profile,* October 2010, pp. 3-4, [online], available at: http://www.ons.gov.uk/ons/search/index.html?pageSize=50&newquery=unlimited+companies+turnover
2   IBID, p. 6
3   BERR, 'UK COMPANY STATISTICS RECONCILIATION PROJECT – Final Report', January 2009, pp. 7-8, Available at: http://www.bis.gov.uk/files/file50753.pdf
4   BERR, 'UK COMPANY STATISTICS RECONCILIATION PROJECT – Final Report', p. 9
5   ONS, 'UK Business: Activity, Size and Location 2011', October 2011, pp. 1-2, available at: http://www.ons.gov.uk/ons/rel/bus-register/uk-business/2011/sum-ukbusiness-2011.html
6   BIS Statistical Release, 'Business Population Estimates for the UK and Regions 2010', May 2011, p.1, available at: http://www.bis.gov.uk/assets/biscore/statistics/docs/b/bpe_2010_stats_release.pdf
7   BIS Statistical Release, 'Business Population Estimates for the UK and Regions 2010', May 2011, pp. 3-4, available at: http://www.bis.gov.uk/assets/biscore/statistics/docs/b/bpe_2010_stats_release.pdf
8   BIS, 'Small Business Survey 2010', April 2011, p. 9, available at: http://www.bis.gov.uk/assets/biscore/enterprise/docs/b/11-p74-bis-small-business-survey-2010
9   BIS, 'Small Business Survey 2010', pp. 15-16

Appendix 2

1   The article is also available online at: http://www.senscot.net/view_art.php?viewid=5024